## THE AUSTRALIAN
# Women's Weekly
# Easy Mexican

A fusion of colour and flavour — the authentic taste of Mexico

**BAUER**

MEDIA GROUP

# CONTENTS

# DRINKS, SNACKS & STARTERS

## fried oysters with salsa

PREP + COOK TIME 35 MINUTES **MAKES** 12

1 small tomato (90g), chopped finely

½ medium yellow capsicum (bell pepper) (100g), chopped finely

½ medium red onion (85g), chopped finely

1 tablespoon finely chopped fresh coriander (cilantro)

1 tablespoon olive oil

1 tablespoon lime juice

1 fresh small red thai (serrano) chilli, seeded, chopped finely

12 oysters on the half shell

½ cup (85g) polenta

⅓ cup (80ml) milk

1 egg, beaten lightly

pinch cayenne pepper

vegetable oil, for deep-frying

1  Preheat oven to 180°C/350°F.

2  To make salsa, combine tomato, capsicum, onion, coriander, olive oil, juice and chilli in a small bowl; season to taste.

3  Remove oysters from shells; reserve oysters. Place shells on an oven tray; heat in oven for 5 minutes.

4  Meanwhile, combine polenta, milk, egg and cayenne pepper in a small bowl.

5  Heat vegetable oil in a medium saucepan. Dip oysters in polenta batter; deep-fry oysters, in batches, until browned lightly. Drain on absorbent paper. Return oysters to shells; top with salsa to serve.

nutritional count per oyster
▶ 5.5g total fat
▶ 1g saturated fat
▶ 276kJ (66 cal)
▶ 6.1g carbohydrate
▶ 2.9g protein
▶ 0.5g fibre

# margarita

**PREP TIME** 5 MINUTES  **SERVES** 1

You can buy sugar syrup from liquor stores or make your own. Stir 1 cup caster (superfine) sugar with 1 cup water in a small saucepan, over low heat, until sugar dissolves; bring to the boil. Reduce heat; simmer, uncovered, without stirring, for 5 minutes. Remove from heat; cool to room temperature. Store in an airtight container in the fridge for up to 1 month. We used Cointreau for this recipe.

2 limes, halved

1 cup ice cubes

45ml (1½ fluid ounces) dark tequila

30ml (1 fluid ounce) orange-flavoured liqueur

30ml (1 fluid ounce) sugar syrup (see above)

**1** Rub one lime half around the rim of a 150ml (4½-fluid ounce) margarita glass; turn the glass upside-down and dip wet rim into a saucer of salt.
**2** Juice the limes (you need 30ml/1 fluid ounce of juice).
**3** Place the ice cubes, tequila, liqueur, juice and syrup in a cocktail shaker; shake vigorously. Strain into glass. Garnish with thin slices of lime rind.

**nutritional count per serving**
▶ 0.2g total fat
▶ 31.4g carbohydrate
▶ 0g saturated fat
▶ 0.3g protein
▶ 1216kJ (291 cal)
▶ 0.1g fibre

# frozen margarita

PREP TIME 5 MINUTES  SERVES 1

You can buy sugar syrup from liquor stores or make your own. Stir 1 cup caster (superfine) sugar with 1 cup water in a small saucepan, over low heat, until sugar dissolves; bring to the boil. Reduce heat; simmer, uncovered, without stirring, for 5 minutes. Remove from heat; cool to room temperature. Store in an airtight container in the fridge for up to 1 month. We used Cointreau for this recipe.

2 limes, halved

1½ cups ice cubes

45ml (1½ fluid ounces) dark tequila

30ml (1 fluid ounce) orange-flavoured liqueur

30ml (1 fluid ounce) sugar syrup (see above)

**1** Rub one lime half around the rim of a 150ml (4½-fluid ounce) margarita glass; turn the glass upside-down and dip wet rim into a saucer of salt.
**2** Juice the limes (you need 30ml/1 fluid ounce of juice).
**3** Blend or process ingredients until smooth. Pour into glass; garnish with fresh mint leaves and slices of lime.

nutritional count per serving
▶ 0.2g total fat
▶ 31.4g carbohydrate
▶ 0g saturated fat
▶ 0.3g protein
▶ 1216kJ (291 cal)
▶ 0.1g fibre

# blood orange margarita

**PREP TIME** 5 MINUTES  **SERVES** 1

You can buy sugar syrup from liquor stores or make your own. Stir 1 cup caster (superfine) sugar with 1 cup water in a small saucepan, over low heat, until sugar dissolves; bring to the boil. Reduce heat; simmer, uncovered, without stirring, for 5 minutes. Remove from heat; cool to room temperature. Store in an airtight container in the fridge for up to 1 month.

2 limes, halved

1 cup ice cubes

45ml (1½ fluid ounces) dark tequila

30ml (1 fluid ounce) blood orange juice

30ml (1 fluid ounce) sugar syrup (see above)

**1** Rub one lime half around the rim of a 260ml (8½-fluid ounce) old-fashioned glass; turn the glass upside-down and dip wet rim into a saucer of salt.
**2** Juice the limes (you need 30ml/1 fluid ounce of juice).
**3** Place the ice cubes, tequila, juices and syrup in a cocktail shaker; shake vigorously. Strain into glass.

**nutritional count per serving**
▶ 0.2g total fat          ▶ 3.07g carbohydrate
▶ 0g saturated fat        ▶ 0.4g protein
▶ 881kJ (210 cal)         ▶ 0.1g fibre

# sangrita

**PREP TIME** 5 MINUTES **SERVES** 4

Not to be confused with 'sangria', the Spanish fruit-laced wine drink, 'sangrita', loosely meaning 'little blood', is a tangy, spicy and refreshing drink traditionally served as a chaser or as an accompaniment to good-quality tequila – ordered as tequila 'completo'. It was designed to be slowly sipped alongside a shooter of tequila, cutting the harshness and cooling the fire of the tequila. Many of us usually associate tequila with the ritual of the 'shot' – taken with a lick of salt and finished with a wedge of lime – but in reality, most true tequila-lover's would not drink tequila as a stand-alone drink. They would rather slowly sip and savour the flavour of the drink, alongside sangrita, to extract its taste.

125ml (4 fluid ounces) chilled tomato juice

80ml (2½ fluid ounces) chilled orange juice

40ml (1½ fluid ounces) lime juice

dash Tabasco

pinch celery salt

pinch onion powder

120ml (4 fluid ounces) tequila

**1** Place juices, tabasco, celery salt and onion powder in a medium jug; mix well. Pour into four 80ml (2½-fluid ounce) tall shot glasses.
**2** Pour tequila into four 30ml (1-fluid ounce) shot glasses; serve sangrita alongside tequila shooters.

nutritional count per serving
▶ 0.4g total fat          ▶ 3.1g carbohydrate
▶ 0g saturated fat        ▶ 0.4g protein
▶ 322kJ (77 cal)          ▶ 0.2g fibre

# mexican coffee

**PREP + COOK TIME** 15 MINUTES **SERVES** 6

1.5 litres (6 cups) water

3 x 5cm (2-inch) strips orange rind

½ cup (45g) coarsely ground coffee beans

¼ cup (55g) raw sugar

¼ cup (55g) firmly packed brown sugar

1 cinnamon stick

6 whole cloves

**1** Bring 1.25 litres (5 cups) of the water to the boil in a medium saucepan; stir in rind, coffee, sugars, cinnamon and cloves. Reduce heat; simmer, uncovered, for 5 minutes. Remove from heat, add remaining water; stand, covered, for 5 minutes.
**2** Strain mixture into a large heatproof jug; pour into coffee cups to serve.

# mexican hot chocolate

**PREP + COOK TIME** 15 MINUTES **SERVES** 6

1 litre (4 cups) milk

3 x 5cm (2-inch) strips orange rind

1 cinnamon stick

185g (6 ounces) dark (semi-sweet) chocolate, chopped finely

**1** Bring milk, rind and cinnamon to the boil in a medium saucepan. Remove from heat; stand, covered, for 5 minutes.
**2** Discard rind and cinnamon. Add chocolate; stir until smooth. Garnish with extra finely grated dark eating chocolate to serve.

*(pictured page 12)*

**nutritional count per serving**
▸ 0g total fat
▸ 18.5g carbohydrate
▸ 0g saturated fat
▸ 0.1g protein
▸ 297kJ (71 cal)
▸ 0.1g fibre

**nutritional count per serving**
▸ 15.3g total fat
▸ 27.4g carbohydrate
▸ 9.5g saturated fat
▸ 7.2g protein
▸ 1133kJ (271 cal)
▸ 0.4g fibre

mexican hot chocolate (recipe page 11)

# shredded pork and bean soup

**PREP + COOK TIME** 2¾ HOURS  **SERVES** 6

1 large carrot (180g), chopped coarsely

1 stalk celery (150g), trimmed, chopped coarsely

5 cloves garlic, unpeeled, bruised

6 black peppercorns

3 sprigs fresh oregano

1 dried bay leaf

1kg (2-pound) piece pork neck

2 litres (8 cups) chicken stock

2 litres (8 cups) water

1 tablespoon olive oil

1 large red onion (300g), chopped coarsely

1 medium red capsicum (bell pepper) (200g), chopped coarsely

1 medium yellow capsicum (bell pepper) (200g), chopped coarsely

2 fresh long red chillies, sliced thinly

2 cloves garlic, crushed

810g (1½ pounds) canned crushed tomatoes

1 teaspoon ground cumin

2 tablespoons coarsely chopped fresh oregano

410g (13 ounces) canned kidney beans, rinsed, drained

**1** Place carrot, celery, bruised garlic, peppercorns, oregano sprigs, bay leaf, pork, stock and the water in a large saucepan; bring to the boil. Reduce heat; simmer, covered, for 1 hour. Uncover; simmer for 1 hour.

**2** Transfer pork to a medium bowl; using two forks, shred pork coarsely. Strain broth through a muslin-lined sieve or colander into a large heatproof bowl; discard solids.

**3** Heat oil in the same cleaned pan; cook onion, capsicums, chilli and crushed garlic, stirring, until vegetables soften.

**4** Return pork and broth to pan with tomatoes, cumin and chopped oregano; bring to the boil. Reduce heat; simmer, covered, for 15 minutes. Add beans; simmer, covered, until soup is hot. Season to taste.

**nutritional count per serving**
▶ 7.4g total fat
▶ 1.6g saturated fat
▶ 1490kJ (356 cal)
▶ 20.8g carbohydrate
▶ 46.5g protein
▶ 9.1g fibre

# chipotle beef tostaditas

**PREP + COOK TIME** 55 MINUTES (+ STANDING) **MAKES** 36

These delicious little bites are fried tortillas
with a beef topping.

2 chipotle chillies

½ cup (125ml) boiling water

12 x 17cm (6¾-inch) round white corn tortillas

vegetable oil, for shallow-frying

1 tablespoon vegetable oil, extra

1 small brown onion (80g), sliced thinly

1 clove garlic, crushed

280g (9 ounces) minced (ground) beef

1 tablespoon tomato paste

1 cup (250ml) beer

¼ cup coarsely chopped fresh coriander (cilantro)

½ cup (120g) sour cream

**1** Cover chillies with the boiling water in a small
heatproof bowl; stand for 20 minutes.
**2** Meanwhile, cut three 7cm (2¾-inch) rounds from
each tortilla. Heat oil in a deep medium frying pan;
shallow-fry rounds, in batches, until browned lightly.
Drain on absorbent paper. Drain oil from pan;
(reserve for another use).
**3** Drain chillies over a small bowl; reserve liquid.
Remove stems from chillies; discard stems. Blend
or process chillies and reserved liquid until smooth.
**4** Heat extra vegetable oil in a medium frying pan;
cook onion, stirring, until softened. Add garlic and
beef; cook, stirring, until beef is changed in colour.
Stir in paste, beer and chilli purée; bring to the boil.
Reduce heat; simmer, uncovered, for 15 minutes or
until liquid is almost evaporated. Stir in coriander.
Season to taste.
**5** Top each tortilla crisp with a rounded teaspoon
of the chipotle beef then with ½ teaspoon of the
sour cream.

**nutritional count per piece**
▶ 3.2g total fat
▶ 1.3g saturated fat
▶ 238kJ (57 cal)
▶ 4.3g carbohydrate
▶ 2.4g protein
▶ 0.6g fibre

# ceviche

**PREP TIME** 15 MINUTES (+ REFRIGERATION) **SERVES** 4

Ceviche, pronounced se-vee-chay, is a Latin-American specialty. You need about 10 limes for this recipe. The lime juice 'cooks' the fish. Fish must be marinated with the lime juice in a non-reactive bowl (one made from glazed porcelain or glass is best), to avoid the metallic taste that can result if marinating takes place in a stainless-steel or an aluminium bowl. Ensure all of the fish is completely covered with juice.

1kg (2 pounds) skinless redfish fillets

1½ cups (375ml) lime juice

¼ cup (40g) pickled sliced jalapeño chillies, drained

¼ cup (60ml) olive oil

250g (8 ounces) mixed baby tomatoes, chopped coarsely

¼ cup finely chopped fresh coriander (cilantro)

1 small red onion (100g), sliced thinly

1 clove garlic, crushed

**1** Discard any skin or bones from fish; cut fish into 2.5cm (1-inch) pieces.
**2** Combine fish and juice in a large glass bowl. Cover; refrigerate overnight.
**3** Drain fish; discard juice. Return fish to bowl, add remaining ingredients; toss gently to combine. Cover; refrigerate for 1 hour. Season to taste.

**nutritional count per serving**
▶ 18.5g total fat
▶ 3.4g saturated fat
▶ 1685kJ (403 cal)
▶ 4g carbohydrate
▶ 52.5g protein
▶ 1.9g fibre

# chile con queso

**PREP + COOK TIME** 20 MINUTES  **MAKES** 2 CUPS

2 teaspoons vegetable oil

½ small green capsicum (bell pepper) (75g), chopped finely

½ small brown onion (40g), chopped finely

1 tablespoon pickled sliced jalapeño chillies, drained, chopped finely

1 clove garlic, crushed

200g (6½ ounces) canned chopped tomatoes

250g (8 ounces) cream cheese, softened

**1** Heat oil in a medium saucepan over medium heat; cook capsicum, onion, chilli and garlic, stirring, for 5 minutes or until onion softens. Add tomatoes; cook, stirring, for 2 minutes.
**2** Add cream cheese; whisk until combined and dip is smooth. Season to taste.
**3** Serve cheese dip hot, accompanied with corn chips, if you like.

**nutritional count per tablespoon**
- 3.9g total fat
- 0.7g carbohydrate
- 2.3g saturated fat
- 1g protein
- 171kJ (41 cal)
- 0.2g fibre

# shredded pork chimichanga

**PREP + COOK TIME** 1¾ HOURS (+ COOLING) **MAKES** 16

Nothing goes better with a jug of margarita or a cold Mexican beer than one of these deep-fried burritos.

500g (1 pound) diced pork

3 cloves garlic

2 black peppercorns

1 teaspoon ground cumin

3 cups (750ml) water

½ cup coarsely chopped fresh coriander (cilantro)

1 small red onion (100g), chopped finely

2 fresh green jalapeño chillies, seeded, chopped finely

8 x 20cm (8-inch) flour tortillas

vegetable oil, for deep-frying

**1** Place pork, garlic, peppercorns, cumin and the water in a large saucepan; bring to the boil. Reduce heat; simmer, covered, for 1 hour or until pork is tender. Cool.

**2** Drain liquid from pork; discard peppercorns and liquid. Shred pork and garlic, using two forks. Combine pork mixture with coriander, onion and chilli in a large bowl; season to taste.

**3** Heat tortillas following directions on the packet. Divide pork mixture evenly between tortillas; roll up firmly, secure with a toothpick at each end.

**4** Heat oil in a large frying pan over high heat; deep-fry tortilla rolls, in batches, until browned lightly. Drain on kitchen paper. Remove toothpicks.

**5** Cut each chimichanga in half; accompany with guacamole (see recipe on page 99).

**nutritional count per piece**
▶ 6.6g total fat
▶ 1.4g saturated fat
▶ 544kJ (130 cal)
▶ 9.1g carbohydrate
▶ 8.2g protein
▶ 0.3g fibre

# tortilla lime soup

PREP + COOK TIME 50 MINUTES  SERVES 4

1 medium white onion (150g), chopped coarsely

2 cloves garlic, quartered

1 fresh long red chilli, chopped coarsely

4 medium tomatoes (600g), peeled, quartered

1 tablespoon peanut oil

¼ teaspoon ground allspice

1½ cups (375ml) chicken stock

1.25 litres (5 cups) water

2 teaspoons finely grated lime rind

¼ cup (60ml) lime juice

¼ cup (70g) tomato paste

⅓ cup (80ml) peanut oil, extra

6 x 15cm (6-inch) corn tortillas, cut into 2cm (¾-inch) wide strips

1 medium avocado (250g), chopped finely

2 green onions (scallions), chopped finely

¼ cup coarsely chopped fresh coriander (cilantro)

1  Blend or process white onion, garlic, chilli and tomato until smooth.

2  Heat oil in a large saucepan; cook tomato mixture and allspice, stirring, until fragrant.

3  Add stock, the water, rind, juice and paste; bring to the boil. Reduce heat; simmer, uncovered, for 15 minutes or until soup thickens. Season to taste.

4  Meanwhile, heat extra oil in a medium frying pan; cook tortilla strips, in batches, until golden. Drain on absorbent paper.

5  Divide tortilla strips into bowls; ladle over soup. Serve topped with combined avocado, green onion and coriander.

**nutritional count per serving**
▶ 33.8g total fat
▶ 6.5g saturated fat
▶ 1764kJ (422 cal)
▶ 20.6g carbohydrate
▶ 6.4g protein
▶ 5.7g fibre

# pork, olive and egg empanadas

PREP + COOK TIME 1 HOUR  MAKES 24

An empanada is a stuffed pastry. You need
2 hard-boiled eggs for this recipe.

1 tablespoon olive oil

1 medium brown onion (150g), chopped finely

½ teaspoon each ground cumin, cinnamon
and smoked paprika

¼ teaspoon each ground nutmeg and cloves

375g (12 ounces) minced (ground) pork

2 hard-boiled eggs, grated coarsely

⅓ cup (40g) pitted black olives, chopped finely

6 sheets shortcrust pastry

1 egg, beaten lightly

lemon wedges, to serve

1  Heat oil in a large frying pan over medium heat;
cook onion, stirring, for 5 minutes or until soft.
Add spices and pork; cook, stirring, over high heat,
until browned. Cool.

2  Stir hard-boiled eggs and olives into pork mixture;
season to taste.

3  Preheat oven to 200°C/400°F. Oil two oven trays.

4  To make empanadas, cut 24 x 12cm (5-inch)
rounds from pastry. Drop heaped tablespoons of
filling onto rounds; brush edges with beaten egg.
Fold rounds in half to enclose filling; pinch edges
to seal.

5  Place empanadas on oven trays with the sealed
edge upright; brush top with beaten egg.

6  Bake empanadas for 25 minutes or until browned
lightly. Serve with lemon wedges.

---

**nutritional count per empanada**

▶ 14g total fat ▶ 19.2g carbohydrate
▶ 6.7g saturated fat ▶ 6.7g protein
▶ 961kJ (230 cal) ▶ 0.9g fibre

# bean nachos

**PREP + COOK TIME** 20 MINUTES **SERVES** 6

810g (1½ pounds) canned kidney beans,
rinsed, drained

⅓ cup (85g) chunky tomato salsa

⅓ cup finely chopped fresh coriander (cilantro)

220g (7 ounces) corn chips

1½ cups (180g) coarsely grated cheddar cheese

2 cups (120g) finely shredded iceberg lettuce

1 small tomato (90g), chopped coarsely

½ small avocado (100g), chopped coarsely

2 tablespoons lime juice

**1** Preheat oven to 220°C/425°F.
**2** Combine half the beans with salsa in a medium
bowl; mash until chunky. Stir in remaining beans
and coriander.
**3** Spread half the chips in a medium shallow
baking dish; top with half the cheese and half the
bean mixture. Top with remaining chips, cheese
then remaining bean mixture. Bake for 10 minutes.
**4** Place lettuce, tomato and avocado in a medium
bowl with juice; toss gently to combine. Season
to taste.
**5** Serve nachos topped with salad.

**nutritional count per serving**
▸ 24.5g total fat          ▸ 33.7g carbohydrate
▸ 11.6g saturated fat      ▸ 17.3g protein
▸ 1856kJ (444 cal)         ▸ 10.8g fibre

# crab tostadas

PREP + COOK TIME 25 MINUTES  SERVES 4

vegetable oil, for shallow-frying

4 x 15cm (6-inch) flour tortillas

410g (13 ounces) canned kidney beans, rinsed, drained, mashed

½ cup (60g) pitted black olives

1 cup (120g) coarsely grated cheddar cheese

1 medium tomato (150g), sliced thinly

1½ cups (90g) shredded iceberg lettuce

170g (5½ ounces) fresh cooked crab meat

AVOCADO CREAM

2 medium avocados (500g), chopped coarsely

2 tablespoons lime juice

½ cup (120g) sour cream

2 green onions (scallions), sliced thinly

1½ tablespoons finely chopped fresh coriander (cilantro)

**1** Make avocado cream.

**2** Heat oil in a medium frying pan; shallow-fry tortillas, one at a time, until browned both sides and crisp. Drain on absorbent paper.

**3** Spread tortillas with avocado cream then mashed beans; top with olives, cheese, tomato, lettuce and crab meat. Season with freshly ground black pepper.

**AVOCADO CREAM** Mash avocado with juice and sour cream in a medium bowl with a fork until well combined; stir in onion and coriander. Season to taste.

**nutritional count per serving**
▶ 44.9g total fat
▶ 19.1g saturated fat
▶ 2554kJ (611 cal)
▶ 26.3g carbohydrate
▶ 22.4g protein
▶ 7.5g fibre

Named after Caesar Cardini, the Italian-American who tossed the first caesar in Mexico during the 1920s, this salad always contains fresh croutons, crisp cos lettuce leaves, lightly boiled eggs, lemon juice, olive oil, worcestershire sauce and parmesan cheese but no single ingredient should dominate.

# classic caesar salad

**PREP + COOK TIME** 45 MINUTES **SERVES** 4

½ loaf ciabatta (220g)

1 clove garlic, crushed

⅓ cup (80ml) olive oil

2 eggs

3 baby cos (romaine) lettuces, leaves separated

1 cup (80g) flaked parmesan cheese

**CAESAR DRESSING**

1 clove garlic, crushed

1 tablespoon dijon mustard

2 tablespoons lemon juice

2 teaspoons worcestershire sauce

2 tablespoons olive oil

1  Preheat oven to 180°C/350°F.

2  Cut bread into 2cm (¾-inch) cubes; combine garlic and oil in a large bowl with bread. Toast bread on an oven tray until croûtons are browned.

3  Make caesar dressing.

4  Bring water to the boil in a small saucepan, add eggs; cover pan tightly, remove from heat. Remove eggs from water after 2 minutes. When cool enough to handle, break eggs into a large bowl; add lettuce, mixing gently so egg coats the leaves.

5  Add cheese, croûtons and dressing to bowl; toss gently to combine. Season to taste.

**CAESAR DRESSING**  Place ingredients in a screw-top jar; shake well to combine.

nutritional count per serving
▸ 39.1g total fat
▸ 9.1g saturated fat
▸ 2366kJ (566 cal)
▸ 33.1g carbohydrate
▸ 18.4g protein
▸ 5.6g fibre

This is our version of huevos rancheros, or ranch-style eggs, which traditionally is made with fried eggs and beans. For extra bite, serve with Tabasco, a fiery sauce made from hot red chillies.

# scrambled eggs with fresh tomato salsa

PREP + COOK TIME 20 MINUTES SERVES 4

3 cured chorizo sausages (500g), sliced thickly

8 eggs

½ cup (125ml) pouring cream

20g (¾ ounce) butter

4 x 15cm (6-inch) flour tortillas

1 cup (120g) coarsely grated cheddar cheese

FRESH TOMATO SALSA

2 small tomatoes (180g), chopped finely

½ small red onion (50g), chopped finely

1 tablespoon red wine vinegar

1 tablespoon olive oil

¼ cup coarsely chopped fresh coriander (cilantro)

1  Preheat oven to 160°C/325°F.

2  Make fresh tomato salsa.

3  Meanwhile, cook chorizo in a medium frying pan over medium-high heat until browned. Drain on absorbent paper; cover to keep warm.

4  Whisk eggs and cream in a medium bowl. Melt butter in cleaned frying pan; cook egg mixture over low heat, stirring gently, until creamy.

5  Meanwhile, place tortillas on an oven tray, sprinkle with cheese; warm in oven until cheese is melted.

6  Divide tortillas between serving plates; top with egg, chorizo and salsa.

**FRESH TOMATO SALSA** Combine tomato, onion, vinegar and oil in a small bowl. Cover; stand for 15 minutes. Stir in coriander just before serving; season to taste.

nutritional count per serving
▶ 81.7g total fat
▶ 35.8g saturated fat
▶ 4126kJ (987 cal)
▶ 16.2g carbohydrate
▶ 48.2g protein
▶ 1.9g fibre

# MAINS

## fish burritos

PREP + COOK TIME 30 MINUTES (+ REFRIGERATION)  MAKES 8

1 cup coarsely chopped fresh coriander (cilantro)

2 teaspoons finely chopped coriander (cilantro) root and stem mixture

1 fresh long red chilli, chopped coarsely

1 clove garlic, quartered

1½ teaspoons sweet paprika

1 teaspoon ground cumin

⅓ cup (80ml) olive oil

800g (1½ ounces) small white fish fillets, halved

8 x 20cm (8-inch) flour tortillas

1 baby cos (romaine) lettuce (180g), leaves separated

1 lebanese cucumber (130g), sliced thinly

LIME BUTTERMILK DRESSING

¼ cup (60ml) buttermilk

1 teaspoon finely grated lime rind

2 teaspoons lime juice

**1** Blend or process the chopped coriander and the root and stem mixture with chilli, garlic, spices and ¼ cup of the oil until smooth. Combine coriander mixture and fish in a large bowl. Cover; refrigerate for 30 minutes.

**2** Meanwhile, make lime buttermilk dressing.

**3** Heat remaining oil in a large frying pan over medium-high heat; cook fish, in batches, until browned both sides and cooked through. Cover to keep warm.

**4** Meanwhile, heat tortillas according to directions on packet.

**5** Divide lettuce, cucumber, fish and dressing between tortillas; wrap firmly to enclose filling.

**LIME BUTTERMILK DRESSING** Combine ingredients in a small jug; season to taste.

nutritional count per burrito
▶ 14g total fat
▶ 2.5g saturated fat
▶ 1267kJ (303 cal)
▶ 19g carbohydrate
▶ 24.3g protein
▶ 2g fibre

# chilli seared tuna with avocado cream and grilled corn

PREP + COOK TIME 1 HOUR (+ STANDING & REFRIGERATION) SERVES 4

4 chipotle chillies

1 tablespoon olive oil

1 small brown onion (80g), chopped finely

2 cloves garlic, crushed

⅓ cup loosely packed fresh oregano leaves

2 tablespoons tomato paste

2 tablespoons water

4 x 200g (6½-ounce) tuna steaks

2 trimmed corn cobs (500g)

8 x 20cm (8-inch) flour tortillas

limes wedges, to serve

### AVOCADO CREAM

2 small avocados (400g), chopped coarsely

½ cup (120g) sour cream

¼ cup coarsely chopped fresh coriander (cilantro)

1 tablespoon lime juice

1  Cover chillies with boiling water in a small heatproof bowl; stand for 20 minutes. Drain chillies; discard stems, chop chillies coarsely.

2  Heat oil in a small frying pan; cook onion and garlic, stirring, until onion softens. Stir in chilli, oregano, paste and the water; bring to the boil. Remove from heat; blend or process mixture, pulsing, until mixture forms thick paste.

3  Place fish, in single layer, in a large shallow dish; using fingers, pat chilli paste onto both sides of fish. Cover; refrigerate for 30 minutes.

4  Meanwhile, make avocado cream.

5  Cook corn on a heated oiled grill plate (or grill or barbecue) until browned lightly and just tender. Remove from heat; slice thickly, cover to keep warm.

6  Cook undrained fish on same heated oiled grill plate until cooked as desired. Cover; stand for 5 minutes. Slice fish thickly.

7  Meanwhile, heat tortillas according to instructions on packet.

8  Divide fish, corn, avocado cream and tortillas between serving plates. Serve with lime wedges.

**AVOCADO CREAM**  Blend or process avocado and sour cream until smooth; stir in coriander and juice. Season to taste.

### nutritional count per serving
▸ 49.6g total fat
▸ 17.5g saturated fat
▸ 3883kJ (929 cal)
▸ 53.8g carbohydrate
▸ 62.7g protein
▸ 8.4g fibre

Ceviche, pronounced se-vee-chay, is a Latin-American specialty. The acids in the citrus marinade slightly cook the very thinly sliced raw seafood. Use the freshest, sashimi-quality fish you can find. Raw fish sold as sashimi has to meet stringent guidelines regarding its handling and treatment after leaving the water. We suggest you seek local advice from authorities before eating any raw seafood.

# salmon ceviche salad

**PREP TIME** 25 MINUTES **SERVES** 4

2 medium oranges (480g)

400g (12½-ounce) piece sashimi-quality salmon, sliced thinly

175g (5½ ounces) watercress, trimmed

ORANGE AND DILL DRESSING

1 tablespoon white wine vinegar

1 tablespoon drained baby capers, rinsed

2 teaspoons finely chopped fresh dill

**1** Segment oranges over a small bowl; reserve ¼ cup orange juice for the dressing.
**2** Make orange and dill dressing.
**3** Combine salmon and half the dressing in a medium bowl; stand for 5 minutes.
**4** Place salmon mixture in a large serving bowl with remaining dressing, watercress and orange segments; toss gently to combine. Season to taste.

**ORANGE AND DILL DRESSING** Place vinegar, capers, dill and reserved orange juice in a screw-top jar; shake well.

**nutritional count per serving**
▶ 7.3g total fat
▶ 1.6g saturated fat
▶ 773kJ (185 cal)
▶ 7.4g carbohydrate
▶ 21g protein
▶ 2.6g fibre

**nutritional count per serving**
▶ 24.1g total fat
▶ 4.4g saturated fat
▶ 2416kJ (578 cal)
▶ 50.6g carbohydrate
▶ 37.8g protein
▶ 12.2g fibre

# char-grilled scallops with corn salsa

**PREP + COOK TIME** 45 MINUTES (+ REFRIGERATION) **SERVES** 4

Soak unshucked corn cobs in a pan of cold water for an hour or so. Pull back the husks without removing them then remove the silk. Brush melted butter over the kernels then re-cover the cob with the husk. Put the corn directly onto a hot barbecue grill for 10 minutes, turning once; the result is delicious.

36 scallops (900g), roe removed

2 cloves garlic, crushed

2 tablespoons lime juice

1 tablespoon olive oil

2 corn cobs (800g), trimmed

200g (6½ ounces) grape tomatoes, halved

1 large avocado (320g), chopped coarsely

1 medium red onion (170g), chopped finely

1 medium green capsicum (bell pepper) (200g), chopped finely

2 fresh small red thai (serrano) chillies, chopped finely

¼ cup coarsely chopped fresh coriander (cilantro)

8 x 15cm (6-inch) white corn tortillas

lime wedges, to serve

**LIME DRESSING**

¼ cup (60ml) lime juice

½ teaspoon ground cumin

2 teaspoons olive oil

**1** Combine scallops, garlic, juice and oil in a large bowl. Cover; refrigerate for 3 hours or overnight.

**2** Make lime dressing.

**3** Cook corn on a heated oiled grill plate (or grill or barbecue) until browned lightly and just tender. When cool enough to handle, cut kernels from cobs. Combine corn kernels in a large bowl with tomato, avocado, onion, capsicum, chilli, coriander and dressing; season to taste.

**4** Cook drained scallops, in batches, on a heated grill plate until browned lightly and cooked as desired. Remove from heat; cover to keep warm.

**5** Using tongs, place tortillas, briefly, one at a time, on grill plate to lightly brown both sides (work quickly as the tortillas will toughen if they are overcooked). Wrap tortillas in a clean tea towel to keep warm.

**6** Serve scallops with corn salsa, tortillas and lime wedges.

**LIME DRESSING** Place ingredients in a screw-top jar; shake well.

# beef burritos

PREP + COOK TIME 55 MINUTES  MAKES 4

1 tablespoon olive oil

1 medium brown onion (150g), chopped finely

1 clove garlic, crushed

1 teaspoon ground cumin

¼ teaspoon chilli powder

500g (1 pound) minced (ground) beef

400g (12½ ounces) canned crushed tomatoes

½ cup (125ml) water

400g (12½ ounces) canned kidney beans, rinsed, drained

4 x 20cm (8-inch) flour tortillas

1 cup (120g) coarsely grated cheddar cheese

1 teaspoon hot paprika

¾ cup (180g) sour cream

¼ cup fresh coriander (cilantro) leaves

**1**  Heat oil in a medium frying pan over high heat; add onion, garlic, cumin and chilli powder. Cook, stirring, for 3 minutes or until onion softens. Add beef; cook, stirring, until browned. Stir in tomatoes, the water and beans; simmer, uncovered, for about 15 minutes or until mixture thickens. Remove from heat; season to taste.

**2**  Preheat oven to 200°C/400°F.

**3**  Divide warm beef filling between tortillas, roll to enclose filling; secure with toothpicks.

**4**  Place filled tortillas on an oiled oven tray; sprinkle with cheese and paprika.

**5**  Bake burritos for 10 minutes or until heated through. Remove toothpicks; serve burritos topped with sour cream, coriander and, if you like, guacamole (see page 99).

---

**nutritional count per burrito**

▶ 45g total fat     ▶ 34.1g carbohydrate

▶ 24g saturated fat     ▶ 42.4g protein

▶ 3022kJ (723 cal)     ▶ 7.3g fibre

# pork and cheese quesadillas

PREP + COOK TIME 50 MINUTES  SERVES 4

1 tablespoon olive oil

500g (1 pound) minced (ground) pork

1 medium green capsicum (bell pepper) (200g), chopped finely

1 fresh long red chilli, chopped finely

1 clove garlic, crushed

½ cup coarsely chopped fresh coriander (cilantro)

8 x 20cm (8-inch) flour tortillas

2 tablespoons olive oil, extra

2 cups (240g) coarsely grated cheddar cheese

**1** Heat oil in a large frying pan; cook pork, stirring, until browned. Add capsicum, chilli and garlic; cook, stirring, until fragrant. Remove from heat; stir in coriander, season to taste.

**2** Brush one side of each tortilla with extra oil. Turn half the tortillas oiled-side down; spread over pork mixture, sprinkle with cheese. Top with remaining tortillas, oiled side up.

**3** Cook quesadillas, in batches, in a heated sandwich press or frying pan until browned lightly. Cut quesadillas into quarters; serve with guacamole (see page 99), if you like.

nutritional count per serving
- 47.5g total fat
- 19g saturated fat
- 3189kJ (763 cal)
- 36.3g carbohydrate
- 46.8g protein
- 2.7g fibre

# chicken enchiladas

PREP + COOK TIME 1 HOUR (+ STANDING)  MAKES 10

3 chipotle chillies

1 cup (250ml) boiling water

500g (1 pound) chicken breast fillets

1 tablespoon vegetable oil

1 large red onion (300g), chopped finely

2 cloves garlic, crushed

1 teaspoon ground cumin

1 tablespoon tomato paste

800g (1½ pounds) canned crushed tomatoes

1 tablespoon finely chopped fresh oregano

⅔ cup (160g) sour cream

1½ cups (240g) coarsely grated cheddar cheese

10 x 15cm (6-inch) flour tortillas

**1** Cover chillies with the boiling water in a small heatproof bowl; stand for 20 minutes. Discard stems from chillies. Blend or process chillies with soaking liquid until smooth.

**2** Meanwhile, place chicken in a medium saucepan of boiling water; return to the boil. Reduce heat; simmer, covered, for 10 minutes or until chicken is cooked through. Remove chicken from poaching liquid; cool 10 minutes. Discard poaching liquid; shred chicken finely.

**3** Preheat oven to 180°C/350°F. Oil a shallow rectangular 3-litre (12-cup) ovenproof dish.

**4** Heat oil in a large frying pan; cook onion, stirring, until softened. Reserve half the onion in a small bowl.

**5** Add garlic and cumin to remaining onion in pan; cook, stirring, until fragrant. Add chilli mixture, tomato paste, tomatoes and oregano; bring to the boil. Reduce heat; simmer, uncovered, for 1 minute. Remove sauce from heat. Season to taste.

**6** Meanwhile, combine shredded chicken, reserved onion, half the sour cream and a third of the cheese in a medium bowl.

**7** Heat tortillas according to instructions on packet. Dip tortillas, one at a time, in tomato sauce in pan; place on board, sauce-side up. Place ¼ cup of the chicken mixture along the edge of each tortilla; roll enchiladas to enclose filling.

**8** Spread ½ cup tomato sauce into dish. Place enchiladas, seam-side down, in dish (they should fit snugly, without overcrowding). Pour remaining tomato sauce over enchiladas; sprinkle with remaining cheese.

**9** Cook enchiladas, in oven, uncovered, for about 15 minutes or until cheese melts and enchiladas are heated through. Serve with the remaining sour cream; sprinkle with coriander (cilantro) leaves, if you like.

nutritional count per enchilada
▶ 20g total fat
▶ 10.5g saturated fat
▶ 1588kJ (379 cal)
▶ 25g carbohydrate
▶ 22.3g protein
▶ 3.3g fibre

Salted cod, also called salt cod, baccala, bacalhau, bacalao and morue, is available from Italian, Spanish and Portuguese delicatessens and some specialty food stores. It needs to be de-salted and rehydrated before use.

# salt cod with roasted tomatoes

**PREP + COOK TIME** 50 MINUTES (+ REFRIGERATION & STANDING) **SERVES** 6

1.5kg (3 pounds) salted cod fillets, skin on

6 large tomatoes (1.3kg)

½ cup (125ml) olive oil

1 medium brown onion (150g), chopped coarsely

2 ancho chillies

¼ cup (60ml) boiling water

500g (1 pound) baby new potatoes, halved

4 medium brown onions (600g), chopped finely

6 cloves garlic, crushed

1 teaspoon smoked paprika

1 cup (150g) pimiento-stuffed green olives

½ cup coarsely chopped fresh flat-leaf parsley

**1** Rinse fish under cold water to remove excess salt. Place fish in a large bowl, cover with cold water; refrigerate, covered, overnight, changing the water three or four times. Drain fish; discard water.

**2** Preheat oven to 200°C/400°F.

**3** Remove cores from tomatoes; cut a small cross in the skin at the base of each tomato. Place on an oiled oven tray, drizzle with 1 tablespoon of the oil; roast for 15 minutes or until tomatoes begin to soften. When cool enough to handle, peel away skins.

**4** Meanwhile, place fish in a large saucepan with coarsely chopped onion, cover with water; bring to the boil. Reduce heat; simmer, uncovered, for 15 minutes or until fish is cooked. Drain fish; discard liquid and onion. Remove skin and bones from fish; flake fish into 4cm (1½-inch) pieces.

**5** Cover chillies with the boiling water in a small heatproof bowl; stand for 20 minutes. Drain chillies; discard stems and seeds, chop chillies coarsely. Blend or process tomatoes and chillies until smooth.

**6** Boil, steam or microwave potato until tender; drain.

**7** Heat remaining oil in a large frying pan; cook the finely chopped onion and garlic, stirring, until onion is softened and browned lightly. Add paprika; cook, stirring, for 1 minute. Add tomato mixture, fish, potato, olives and parsley; season to taste, stir gently until heated through.

**nutritional count per serving**
▶ 3.8g total fat
▶ 0.6g saturated fat
▶ 589kJ (141 cal)
▶ 3.1g carbohydrate
▶ 22.7g protein
▶ 1.2g fibre

# chicken mole

PREP + COOK TIME 1½ HOURS  SERVES 6

6 x 500g (1-pound) small chickens

⅓ cup (50g) plain (all-purpose) flour

¼ cup (60ml) olive oil

1 medium brown onion (150g), chopped finely

2 fresh long red chillies, sliced thinly

2 cloves garlic, crushed

1 cinnamon stick

½ teaspoon ground nutmeg

¼ teaspoon ground cloves

800g (1½ pounds) canned crushed tomatoes

1 large red capsicum (bell pepper) (350g), sliced thinly

1 cup (250ml) dry white wine

60g (2 ounces) dark (semi-sweet) chocolate, chopped finely

⅓ cup coarsely chopped fresh flat-leaf parsley

1 Rinse chickens under cold water; pat dry with absorbent paper. Using kitchen scissors, cut along both sides of chickens' backbones; discard backbones. Halve chickens along the breastbones then cut each half into two pieces.

2 Coat chicken in flour; shake off excess. Heat oil in a large frying pan over high heat; cook chicken, in batches, until browned. Drain on absorbent paper.

3 Cook onion, chilli and garlic in the same pan, stirring, over medium heat, for 5 minutes or until onion softens. Add spices to pan; cook, stirring, for 30 seconds or until fragrant.

4 Return chicken to pan with tomatoes, capsicum and wine; simmer, covered, for 20 minutes. Uncover; simmer for 20 minutes or until chicken is tender and sauce thickens slightly.

5 Add chocolate; cook, stirring, until sauce is smooth. Season to taste. Discard cinnamon stick. Serve chicken with sauce; sprinkle with parsley.

**SERVING SUGGESTION** Serve with steamed green beans and rice or a green salad, and crusty bread to mop up the juices.

nutritional count per serving
▶ 51.9g total fat
▶ 15.3g saturated fat
▶ 3294kJ (788 cal)
▶ 20.1g carbohydrate
▶ 52.8g protein
▶ 3.3g fibre

# marinated chilli chickens

**PREP + COOK TIME** 1½ HOURS (+ REFRIGERATION) **SERVES** 8

4 x 500g (1-pound) small chickens

2 small brown onions (200g), chopped coarsely

8 cloves garlic, peeled

8 fresh long red chillies

⅓ cup (80ml) red wine vinegar

1 tablespoon ground cumin

2 tablespoons olive oil

4 medium ripe tomatoes (750g), quartered

**1** Rinse chickens under cold water; pat dry with absorbent paper. Using kitchen scissors, cut along sides of chickens' backbones; discard backbones. Halve chickens along breastbones.

**2** Blend or process onion, garlic, chillies, vinegar and cumin until almost smooth.

**3** Heat oil in a large frying pan, add onion mixture; cook, stirring, until fragrant.

**4** Blend or process tomatoes until smooth, add to onion mixture; cook, stirring, until mixture boils. Reduce heat; simmer, uncovered, stirring, for 20 minutes or until thickened. Season to taste. Brush chickens with half the chilli sauce; cover, refrigerate for 3 hours.

**5** Preheat oven to 220°C/425°F.

**6** Place chickens, skin-side up, on an oiled wire rack in a large shallow baking dish; roast for about 30 minutes or until cooked through.

**7** Serve chicken with remaining chilli sauce and, if you like, green salad leaves, and grilled corn and zucchini salsa (see page 94).

**nutritional count per serving**
▸ 19.3g total fat
▸ 5.1g saturated fat
▸ 1300kJ (311 cal)
▸ 3.6g carbohydrate
▸ 29.7g protein
▸ 2g fibre

# chicken in pumpkin seed and tomatillo sauce

PREP + COOK TIME 1 HOUR  SERVES 6

2 medium tomatoes (300g), quartered

1 medium brown onion (150g), quartered

2 tablespoons olive oil

6 chicken thigh cutlets (1.2kg)

6 chicken drumsticks (900g)

1½ cups (375ml) chicken stock

1 cup (200g) pumpkin seed kernels (pepitas), roasted

2 tablespoons pickled sliced jalapeño chillies, drained

½ cup (125g) drained, chopped tomatillos

2 cloves garlic, quartered

½ cup firmly packed fresh coriander leaves (cilantro)

⅓ cup coarsely chopped fresh chives

½ teaspoon ground cumin

1 Preheat oven to 200°C/400°F.

2 Place tomato and onion on an oiled oven tray; drizzle with half the oil. Roast, uncovered, for 25 minutes or until vegetables soften. Cool.

3 Meanwhile, place chicken in a large saucepan with stock; bring to the boil. Reduce heat; simmer, covered, for 20 minutes or until chicken is just cooked through. Remove chicken from pan; reserve 1¼ cups of stock.

4 Blend or process pumpkin seed kernels into a fine powder; sift powder through a fine sieve. Blend or process pumpkin seed powder with tomato and onion mixture, chilli, tomatillos, garlic, coriander, chives and cumin until smooth.

5 Heat remaining oil in same cleaned pan; cook chicken, in batches, until browned. Remove from pan. Add pumpkin seed mixture to pan; cook, stirring, for 3 minutes. Add reserved stock; simmer, uncovered, for 2 minutes. Return chicken to pan; simmer, uncovered, until chicken is heated through. Season to taste.

**SERVING SUGGESTION** Serve with steamed rice, lime wedges and fresh coriander leaves.

**NOTE** A tomatillo is a small green fruit that is a member of the tomato family. It is a basic ingredient in Mexican cooking and adds a tart flavour to food. It is covered by a papery husk, similar to that of an onion, which should be removed, as it is not edible. Tomatillos are also available canned.

---

**nutritional count per serving**
- 52g total fat
- 13g saturated fat
- 2959kJ (708 cal)
- 8.6g carbohydrate
- 50.1g protein
- 5g fibre

# chicken in almond pomegranate sauce

PREP + COOK TIME 35 MINUTES  SERVES 4

Pomegranate pulp consists of the seeds and the edible pulp surrounding them; it has a tangy sweet-sour flavour.

2 medium pomegranates (640g)

1½ cups (375ml) water

⅓ cup (75g) firmly packed brown sugar

2 tablespoons olive oil

4 x 200g (6½-ounce) chicken breast fillets

1 large brown onion (200g), sliced thickly

2 cloves garlic, crushed

1 tablespoon plain (all-purpose) flour

1 teaspoon each ground cumin, coriander and sweet paprika

½ teaspoon ground cinnamon

pinch chilli powder

½ cup (125ml) chicken stock

⅓ cup (55g) blanched almonds, roasted

⅓ cup coarsely chopped fresh coriander (cilantro)

1 Cut pomegranates in half, scoop out pulp. Reserve about ⅓ cup pulp. Place remaining pulp in a small saucepan with the water and sugar; stir over medium heat, without boiling, until sugar dissolves. Simmer, uncovered, for 5 minutes; strain syrup into a medium heatproof jug.

2 Heat half the oil in a large frying pan; cook chicken, in batches, until browned. Remove from pan.

3 Heat remaining oil in same pan; cook onion and garlic, stirring, until onion softens. Add flour and spices; cook, stirring, for 1 minute or until mixture is just browned and dry. Gradually stir in stock and pomegranate syrup; cook, stirring, until mixture boils and thickens slightly.

4 Return chicken to pan; simmer, covered, for 5 minutes or until chicken is cooked through. Stir in reserved pomegranate pulp, nuts and coriander; season to taste.

nutritional count per serving
▸ 28g total fat
▸ 5.3g saturated fat
▸ 2366kJ (566 cal)
▸ 29.3g carbohydrate
▸ 47.8g protein
▸ 4.8g fibre

# albondigas

PREP + COOK TIME 50 MINUTES  SERVES 4

Meaning 'meatballs', this can be made into a child-friendly (and non-Mexican) alternative: just delete the chilli and serve the meatballs with pasta.

2 tablespoons vegetable oil

1 medium brown onion (150g), chopped finely

1 clove garlic, crushed

1 teaspoon each ground cumin and coriander

½ teaspoon chilli powder

750g (1½ pounds) minced (ground) beef

800g (1½ pounds) canned crushed tomatoes

410g (13 ounces) canned mexican-style beans

⅓ cup (80g) sour cream

⅓ cup loosely packed fresh coriander leaves (cilantro)

**1** Heat half the oil in a large frying pan over medium heat; cook onion, garlic and spices, stirring, about 5 minutes or until onion softens. Cool.

**2** Combine beef with onion mixture in a medium bowl; season. Using hands, roll level tablespoons of mixture into balls.

**3** Heat remaining oil in the same pan over high heat; cook meatballs, in batches, until browned all over. Remove from pan.

**4** Add tomato and beans to same pan; bring to the boil. Reduce heat; simmer, uncovered, for 5 minutes or until mixture thickens slightly. Return meatballs to pan; simmer, uncovered, for about 10 minutes or until meatballs are cooked through. Season to taste.

**5** Serve meatballs with sour cream, coriander and, if you like, guacamole (see page 99).

**TIPS** Serve with flour tortillas to scoop up the sauce. The meatballs and sauce can be made a day ahead and refrigerated, covered separately.

**nutritional count per serving**
- ▶ 32.2g total fat
- ▶ 13.4g saturated fat
- ▶ 2349kJ (562 cal)
- ▶ 20.4g carbohydrate
- ▶ 44.6g protein
- ▶ 7.8g fibre

# blackened steak salad

PREP + COOK TIME 30 MINUTES  SERVES 4

4 x 15cm (6-inch) flour tortillas

500g (1-pound) beef fillet

¼ teaspoon each dried oregano and thyme

2 teaspoons hot paprika

1 teaspoon ground black pepper

½ teaspoon cayenne pepper

3 medium tomatoes (450g), chopped finely

1 large green capsicum (bell pepper) (350g), chopped finely

1 lebanese cucumber (130g), seeded, chopped finely

½ cup coarsely chopped fresh mint

1 tablespoon olive oil

1 tablespoon balsamic vinegar

1 clove garlic, crushed

lime wedges, to serve

**1** Cook tortillas on a heated oiled grill plate (or grill or barbecue) until browned lightly both sides. Break into coarse pieces.

**2** Rub beef with combined herbs and spices, season. Cook on a heated oiled grill plate (or grill or barbecue), turning, until browned and cooked as desired. Cover beef; stand for 5 minutes then slice thinly.

**3** Place beef and tortilla pieces in a large bowl with remaining ingredients; toss gently to combine, season to taste. Serve with lime wedges.

---

**nutritional count per serving**

▶ 13.7g total fat    ▶ 14.5g carbohydrate

▶ 4g saturated fat    ▶ 30.6g protein

▶ 1304kJ (312 cal)    ▶ 3.4g fibre

# chilli con carne

PREP + COOK TIME 3¾ HOURS (+ STANDING) SERVES 8

1 cup (200g) dried kidney beans

1.5kg (3 pounds) beef chuck steak

2 litres (8 cups) water

1 tablespoon olive oil

2 medium brown onions (300g), chopped coarsely

2 cloves garlic, crushed

2 teaspoons each ground coriander, cumin and sweet paprika

½ teaspoon cayenne pepper

800g (1½ pounds) canned crushed tomatoes

2 tablespoons tomato paste

4 green onions (scallions), chopped coarsely

2 tablespoons coarsely chopped fresh coriander (cilantro)

⅓ cup (65g) finely chopped pickled jalapeño chillies

1  Place beans in a medium bowl, cover with water; stand overnight. Drain.

2  Place beef and the water in a large saucepan; bring to the boil. Reduce heat; simmer, covered, 1½ hours.

3  Drain beef in a large muslin-lined strainer over a large heatproof bowl; reserve 3½ cups of the cooking liquid. Using two forks, shred beef.

4  Heat oil in the same pan over medium heat; cook brown onion and garlic, stirring, for 5 minutes or until onion softens. Add spices; cook, stirring, for 30 seconds or until fragrant. Add beans, tomatoes, paste and 2 cups of the reserved cooking liquid; bring to the boil. Reduce heat; simmer, covered, 1 hour.

5  Add beef and remaining reserved cooking liquid to the pan; simmer, covered, for 30 minutes or until beans are tender. Remove from heat; stir in green onions, coriander and chilli. Season to taste.

**SERVING SUGGESTION** Serve with steamed rice; top with thinly sliced white onion and fresh coriander leaves.

nutritional count per serving
▶ 11.5g total fat
▶ 4g saturated fat
▶ 1513kJ (362 cal)
▶ 15.1g carbohydrate
▶ 45.4g protein
▶ 7.8g fibre

nutritional count per serving
▶ 21.7g total fat
▶ 10g saturated fat
▶ 2169kJ (519 cal)
▶ 57g carbohydrate
▶ 19.8g protein
▶ 8.6g fibre

A quesadilla (from queso, the Spanish word for cheese) is a tortilla 'sandwich' containing cheese and any of a wide number of spicy filling ingredients. It is grilled, fried or toasted and is usually served with salsa. We cooked these quesadillas in a frying pan, but you can cook quesadillas, one at a time, in a heated sandwich press if you have one.

# corn and goat's cheese quesadillas

**PREP + COOK TIME** 30 MINUTES **SERVES** 4

2 corn cobs (800g), trimmed

240g (7½ ounces) soft goat's cheese

8 x 20cm (8-inch) flour tortillas

½ cup (100g) drained char-grilled red capsicum (bell pepper), sliced thinly

2 tablespoons pickled, sliced jalapeño chillies, drained

⅓ cup coarsely chopped fresh coriander (cilantro)

20g (¾ ounce) butter

40g (1½ ounces) baby spinach leaves

lime wedges, to serve

**1** Cook corn on a heated oiled grill plate (or grill or barbecue) until browned lightly and tender; when cool enough to handle, cut kernels from cobs.

**2** Spread cheese over tortillas. Top four of the tortillas with corn, capsicum, chilli and coriander, season; top with remaining tortillas. Press around edges firmly to seal.

**3** Melt butter in a medium frying pan over medium heat; cook quesadillas, one at a time, until browned both sides and heated through.

**4** Serve quesadillas with spinach and lime wedges.

# lamb shanks in chilli sauce

**PREP + COOK TIME** 2½ HOURS (+ STANDING) **SERVES** 4

3 ancho chillies

1 cup (250ml) boiling water

1 tablespoon olive oil

8 french-trimmed lamb shanks (2kg)

1 medium brown onion (150g), chopped finely

3 cloves garlic, crushed

1 teaspoon ground cumin

½ teaspoon ground coriander

2 sprigs fresh thyme

1 litre (4 cups) beef stock

2 cups (500ml) water, extra

2 dried bay leaves

⅓ cup loosely packed fresh coriander leaves (cilantro)

lime wedges, to serve

1  Cover chillies with the boiling water in a small heatproof bowl; stand for 20 minutes. Discard stems and seeds from chillies; blend or process chillies with soaking liquid until smooth.

2  Heat oil in a large saucepan; cook lamb, in batches, until browned. Remove from pan; drain on absorbent paper.

3  Drain fat from pan, add onion and garlic to same pan; cook, stirring, until onion softens. Add spices and chilli mixture; cook, stirring, until fragrant.

4  Return lamb to pan with thyme, stock, the extra water and bay leaves; bring to the boil. Reduce heat; simmer, covered, for 1½ hours or until lamb is tender and almost falling off the bone, skimming fat from the surface occasionally. Uncover; simmer for 20 minutes or until sauce thickens slightly. Discard thyme and bay leaves; season to taste.

5  Divide lamb between serving bowls; top with coriander. Accompany with lime wedges, and fresh crusty bread, if you like.

**nutritional count per serving**
▶ 9.7g total fat
▶ 3.2g saturated fat
▶ 1559kJ (373 cal)
▶ 4.9g carbohydrate
▶ 65.3g protein
▶ 1.1g fibre

nutritional count per serving
▶ 49.8g total fat
▶ 20.4g saturated fat
▶ 5158kJ (1234 cal)
▶ 96.2g carbohydrate
▶ 92g protein
▶ 21.4g fibre

Pasilla (pah-SEE-yah) chillies, also known as 'chile negro' because of their dark brown colour, are the wrinkled, dried version of fresh chilaca chillies. About 20cm (8 inches) in length, a pasilla is only mildly hot, but possesses a rich flavour that adds a smoky depth to the overall recipe.

# spiced grilled beef with chilli beans

**PREP + COOK TIME** 1¾ HOURS (+ STANDING) **SERVES** 4

2 cups (400g) dried black beans

2 pasilla chillies (10g)

¼ cup (60ml) boiling water

2 tablespoons olive oil

1 medium brown onion (150g), chopped finely

3 cloves garlic, crushed

¼ cup (70g) tomato paste

4 medium tomatoes (600g), chopped coarsely

½ cup (125ml) water

2 tablespoons lime juice

2 tablespoons brown sugar

1 tablespoon dried marjoram

2 teaspoons smoked paprika

1kg (2 pounds) beef rump steak

8 x 20cm (8-inch) flour tortillas

1 small red onion (100g), sliced thinly

1 small iceberg lettuce, trimmed, shredded finely

⅓ cup firmly packed fresh coriander leaves (cilantro)

⅔ cup (160g) sour cream

**1** Place beans in a medium bowl, cover with water; stand overnight, drain.

**2** Cook beans in a large saucepan of boiling water, uncovered, until tender; drain. Rinse under cold water; drain.

**3** Meanwhile, cover chillies with the boiling water in a small heatproof bowl; stand for 20 minutes. Discard stalks from chillies. Blend or process chillies with soaking liquid until mixture is smooth.

**4** Heat half the oil in a large saucepan over high heat; cook brown onion and garlic, stirring, for 3 minutes or until onion softens. Add chilli mixture, paste, tomato, the water, juice and sugar; bring to the boil. Remove from heat; blend or process mixture until smooth.

**5** Return chilli mixture to pan; add beans, simmer, covered, for 20 minutes. Uncover; simmer for about 10 minutes or until sauce thickens. Season to taste.

**6** Meanwhile, combine marjoram, paprika and the remaining oil in a large bowl; add beef, turn to coat in mixture, season. Cook beef on a heated oiled grill plate (or grill or barbecue) until browned both sides and cooked as desired. Cover beef; stand for 10 minutes, then slice thinly.

**7** Meanwhile, heat tortillas according to directions on packet. Serve tortillas topped with chilli beans, red onion, lettuce, beef, coriander and sour cream.

Black beans, also known as turtle beans, are a common ingredient in Caribbean and Latin American soups, salsas and salads. They are not the same as chinese black beans, which are fermented soya beans. Black beans are available from greengrocers and delicatessens.

# chilli lamb roasts with black bean salad

PREP + COOK TIME 1½ HOURS (+ STANDING & REFRIGERATION) SERVES 4

1 cup (200g) dried black beans

2 mini lamb roasts (700g)

¼ cup (60ml) olive oil

1 large brown onion (200g), chopped finely

1 clove garlic, crushed

1 fresh long green chilli, chopped finely

1 teaspoon ground cumin

2 tablespoons red wine vinegar

1 large tomato (220g), seeded, chopped coarsely

½ cup firmly packed fresh coriander leaves (cilantro)

3 green onions (scallions), sliced thinly

2 tablespoons lime juice

## CHILLI MARINADE

3 fresh long green chillies, chopped finely

3 green onions (scallions), chopped finely

2 cloves garlic, crushed

1 teaspoon each ground allspice and dried thyme

1 teaspoon white (granulated) sugar

1 tablespoon worcestershire sauce

1 tablespoon lime juice

1 Place beans in a medium bowl, cover with water; stand overnight.

2 Combine ingredients for chilli marinade in a large bowl; add lamb, rub all over with marinade. Cover; refrigerate overnight.

3 Preheat oven to 180°C/350°F.

4 Drain beans; rinse under cold water. Cook beans in a medium saucepan of boiling water, uncovered, for 20 minutes or until tender; drain.

5 Meanwhile, heat half the oil in a medium flameproof casserole dish over high heat on the stove top; cook lamb until browned all over. Transfer to oven; roast lamb, uncovered, for 20 minutes or until cooked as desired. Cover lamb; stand for 10 minutes, then slice thickly.

6 Meanwhile, heat remaining oil in a medium saucepan over medium heat; cook brown onion, garlic, chilli and cumin, stirring, for 5 minutes or until onion softens. Add vinegar; cook, stirring, until liquid evaporates. Remove from heat.

7 Combine the onion mixture, beans, tomato, coriander, green onion and juice in a large bowl; season to taste. Serve lamb with salad.

nutritional count per serving
▶ 30.2g total fat
▶ 9g saturated fat
▶ 2353kJ (563 cal)
▶ 22.4g carbohydrate
▶ 49.8g protein
▶ 12.8g fibre

# lamb fajitas

PREP + COOK TIME 45 MINUTES  SERVES 4

600g (1¼ pounds) lamb strips

3 cloves garlic, crushed

¼ cup (60ml) lemon juice

2 teaspoons ground cumin

1 tablespoon olive oil

1 large red capsicum (bell pepper) (350g), sliced thickly

1 large green capsicum (bell pepper) (350g), sliced thickly

1 medium yellow capsicum (bell pepper) (200g), sliced thickly

1 large red onion (300g), sliced thickly

8 x 20cm (8-inch) flour tortillas

## GUACAMOLE

1 large avocado (320g), chopped coarsely

¼ cup finely chopped fresh coriander (cilantro)

1 tablespoon lime juice

1 small white onion (80g), chopped finely

## SALSA CRUDA

2 medium tomatoes (300g), seeded, chopped finely

1 fresh long green chilli, chopped finely

½ cup coarsely chopped fresh coriander (cilantro)

1 clove garlic, crushed

1 small white onion (80g), chopped finely

2 tablespoons lime juice

**1** Combine lamb, garlic, juice, cumin and oil in a large bowl. Cover; refrigerate.

**2** Make guacamole.

**3** Make salsa cruda.

**4** Cook lamb, in batches, in a heated oiled frying pan over high heat, stirring, until browned all over and cooked as desired. Remove from pan. Cover to keep warm.

**5** Cook capsicums and onion, in batches, in same pan over medium heat, stirring, until just softened. Remove mixture from pan.

**6** Meanwhile, heat tortillas according to directions on packet.

**7** Return lamb and capsicum mixture to pan; stir gently over medium heat until hot.

**8** Serve lamb mixture with tortillas, guacamole and salsa cruda.

**GUACAMOLE** Combine ingredients in a small bowl; season to taste.

**SALSA CRUDA** Combine ingredients in a small bowl; season to taste.

**nutritional count per serving**
- 37.5g total fat
- 10.4g saturated fat
- 3227kJ (772 cal)
- 62.3g carbohydrate
- 45.8g protein
- 8.4g fibre

Prunes, surprisingly, feature in a number of Mexican recipes, so we've made a prune sauce to go with the pork in this recipe. It is reminiscent of the Mexican chilli sauce known as 'mole': these can feature many different ingredients, according to the whim of the cook, including chocolate, but the one ingredient they all feature is chilli.

roast pork with prune sauce (recipe page 70)

# roast pork with prune sauce

PREP + COOK TIME 2 HOURS (+ STANDING) SERVES 8

2kg (4-pound) boneless loin of pork, rind on

### STUFFING

1 tablespoon olive oil

1 medium brown onion (150g), chopped finely

2 cloves garlic, crushed

2 medium tomatoes (300g), seeded, chopped finely

½ cup (75g) raisins

½ cup (80g) blanched almonds, chopped finely

150g (4½ ounces) minced (ground) pork

150g (4½ ounces) minced (ground) veal

1 cup (70g) stale breadcrumbs

### PRUNE SAUCE

1 medium brown onion (150g), quartered

1 medium tomato (150g), quartered

3 cloves garlic, unpeeled

2 tablespoons olive oil

2 chipotle chillies

⅓ cup (55g) blanched almonds

¾ cup (125g) seeded prunes

4 whole cloves

1 teaspoon ground cinnamon

2 tablespoons cider vinegar

1 cup (250ml) chicken stock

*(pictured page 69)*

1 Make stuffing.

2 Preheat oven to 220°C/425°F.

3 Place pork, fat-side down, on board; slice through the thickest part of the pork horizontally, without cutting through to the other side. Open pork out to form one large piece. Press stuffing mixture along one long side of the pork; roll pork to enclose stuffing. Tie pork with kitchen string at 2cm (¾-inch) intervals; place pork on a wire rack in a large shallow baking dish. Roast pork, uncovered, for 30 minutes.

4 Reduce oven temperature to 200°C/400°F. Cover pork; roast for 1 hour or until cooked through.

5 Meanwhile, make prune sauce.

6 Remove pork from dish; cover loosely with foil, stand for 15 minutes then slice thinly.

7 Serve pork with prune sauce.

**STUFFING** Heat oil in a large frying pan; cook onion and garlic, stirring, until onion softens. Add tomato, raisins and nuts; simmer, uncovered, for 5 minutes or until thick. Cool. Combine tomato mixture, minced pork and veal, and breadcrumbs in a medium bowl, season; mix well.

**PRUNE SAUCE** Place onion, tomato and garlic on an oiled oven tray; drizzle with half the oil. Roast, uncovered, in a 200°C/400°F oven, with the pork, for 25 minutes or until vegetables soften. When cool enough to handle, peel tomato and garlic. Meanwhile, remove stems, seeds and membranes from chillies; chop chillies coarsely. Cover chillies with boiling water in a small heatproof bowl; stand for 20 minutes. Drain. Heat remaining oil in a large frying pan; cook nuts, prunes and spices, stirring, until nuts are browned lightly. Blend or process nut mixture and vinegar until mixture forms a thick paste. Add drained chillies, onion, tomato and garlic; process until smooth. Add chilli mixture and stock to same heated pan; simmer, stirring occasionally, until sauce is heated through. Season to taste.

**nutritional count per serving**
▶ 33.4g total fat
▶ 7.5g saturated fat
▶ 2796kJ (669 cal)
▶ 23.6g carbohydrate
▶ 66.9g protein
▶ 4.9g fibre

# barbecued corn with chunky salsa and rice

PREP + COOK TIME 50 MINUTES  SERVES 4

4 untrimmed corn cobs (1.6kg)

2 teaspoons peanut oil

2 cloves garlic, crushed

1 small white onion (80g), chopped finely

1 small red capsicum (bell pepper) (150g), chopped finely

1 fresh long red chilli, chopped finely

1½ cups (300g) white medium-grain rice

1 cup (250ml) vegetable stock

1 cup (250ml) water

CHUNKY SALSA

3 medium tomatoes (450g), chopped coarsely

1 small white onion (80g), chopped finely

¼ cup (60g) pickled, sliced jalapeño chillies, drained

½ cup coarsely chopped fresh coriander (cilantro)

1 clove garlic, crushed

2 tablespoons lime juice

1  Gently peel the husk down the corn cob, keeping it attached at the base. Remove as much of the silk as possible then bring the husk back over the cob to re-wrap and enclose completely. Place corn in a large bowl; add enough cold water to completely submerge the corn.

2  Heat oil in a medium saucepan; cook garlic, onion, capsicum and chilli, stirring, until onion softens. Add rice; cook, stirring, for 1 minute. Add stock and the water; bring to the boil. Reduce heat; simmer, covered, for 20 minutes or until rice is just tender. Remove from heat; fluff rice with a fork, season to taste.

3  Meanwhile, drain corn. Cook corn on a heated oiled grill plate (or grill or barbecue) for 25 minutes or until corn is tender, turning occasionally.

4  Make chunky salsa. Serve corn with rice and salsa.

CHUNKY SALSA  Combine ingredients in a medium bowl; season to taste.

nutritional count per serving
▶ 6.7g total fat
▶ 0.9g saturated fat
▶ 2541kJ (608 cal)
▶ 114g carbohydrate
▶ 20.6g protein
▶ 16.9g fibre

nutritional count per serving
▶ 58g total fat
▶ 28.9g saturated fat
▶ 2867kJ (686 cal)
▶ 19.1g carbohydrate
▶ 19.1g protein
▶ 4.4g fibre

# mushroom crêpes with coriander sauce

PREP + COOK TIME 1½ HOURS (+ STANDING)  SERVES 6

3 eggs

¼ teaspoon salt

⅔ cup (100g) plain (all-purpose) flour

1½ cups (375ml) milk

2 tablespoons olive oil

¾ cup (90g) coarsely grated cheddar cheese

MUSHROOM FILLING

20g (¾ ounce) butter

2 tablespoons olive oil

1 medium brown onion (150g), chopped finely

4 cloves garlic, crushed

1 fresh long red chilli, chopped finely

500g (1 pound) button mushrooms, chopped finely

¼ cup finely chopped fresh coriander (cilantro)

CORIANDER SAUCE

1 tablespoon olive oil

1 large brown onion (200g), chopped finely

4 cloves garlic, crushed

1 cup (250ml) pouring cream

½ cup (120g) sour cream

¾ cup finely chopped fresh coriander (cilantro)

½ cup (60g) coarsely grated cheddar cheese

1  Whisk eggs, salt, flour, milk and oil in a medium bowl until smooth. Cover; stand for 30 minutes.

2  Meanwhile, make mushroom filling.

3  Heat an oiled heavy-based crêpe pan or small frying pan; pour ¼ cup of batter into pan, tilting pan to coat the base. Cook crêpe, over low heat, until browned lightly, loosening the edge of the crêpe with a spatula. Turn crêpe; brown the other side. Remove crêpe from pan; cover to keep warm. Repeat with remaining batter to make a total of 12 crêpes.

4  Preheat oven to 180°C/350°F.

5  Place heaped tablespoons of filling along centre of each crêpe; roll crêpes to enclose filling. Place crêpes, in a single layer, in an oiled shallow baking dish; top with cheese.

6  Bake crêpes in oven for 15 minutes or until filling is hot and cheese is browned lightly.

7  Meanwhile, make coriander sauce. Serve crêpes with sauce.

MUSHROOM FILLING  Heat butter and oil in a large frying pan; cook onion, garlic and chilli, stirring, until onion softens. Add mushrooms; cook, stirring, for 15 minutes or until mushrooms are soft and water has evaporated. Cool slightly; stir in coriander, season to taste.

CORIANDER SAUCE  Heat oil in a large frying pan; cook onion and garlic, stirring, until onion softens. Add cream; simmer, uncovered, for 10 minutes or until thickened. Remove from heat; stir in sour cream, coriander and cheese. Season to taste.

# black bean, corn and chipotle stew

PREP + COOK TIME 1¼ HOURS (+ STANDING)  SERVES 4

1½ cups (300g) dried black beans

2 chipotle chillies

½ cup (125ml) boiling water

1 tablespoon cumin seeds

2 corn cobs (800g), trimmed

2 teaspoons olive oil

1 large brown onion (200g), chopped finely

800g (1½ pounds) canned crushed tomatoes

8 x 15cm (6-inch) white corn tortillas

## SALSA FRESCA

1 small red onion (100g), chopped coarsely

1 small tomato (90g), chopped coarsely

½ cup coarsely chopped fresh coriander (cilantro)

1 lebanese cucumber (130g), chopped coarsely

1 tablespoon olive oil

2 tablespoons lemon juice

1  Place beans in a medium bowl, cover with water; stand overnight, drain. Rinse under cold water; drain.

2  Cook beans in a medium saucepan of boiling water for 15 minutes or until just tender. Drain.

3  Preheat oven to 200°C/400°F.

4  Cover chillies with the boiling water in a small heatproof bowl; stand for 20 minutes. Discard stems; blend or process chilli and soaking liquid until smooth.

5  Dry-fry cumin seeds in a small frying pan, stirring, until fragrant.

6  Cook corn on a heated oiled grill plate (or grill or barbecue) until browned lightly and just tender. When cool enough to handle, cut corn kernels from cobs.

7  Heat oil in a large flameproof dish over medium heat; cook onion, stirring, for 5 minutes or until softened. Add drained beans, chilli mixture, cumin seeds, tomatoes and half the corn; bring to the boil. Transfer to oven; bake, uncovered, for 20 minutes or until sauce thickens. Season to taste.

8  Meanwhile, heat tortillas according to directions on packet.

9  Make salsa fresca. Serve stew with tortillas and salsa.

SALSA FRESCA  Combine remaining corn with salsa ingredients in a medium bowl; season.

## nutritional count per serving
▶ 10.4g total fat
▶ 1.3g saturated fat
▶ 1839kJ (440 cal)
▶ 61.3g carbohydrate
▶ 26.2g protein
▶ 19.5g fibre

# spicy chicken tacos

PREP + COOK TIME 25 MINUTES  MAKES 10

To add extra heat, serve some pickled sliced jalapeno chillies with the tacos.

1 tablespoon olive oil

1 medium brown onion (150g), chopped finely

500g (1 pound) minced (ground) chicken

35g (1 ounce) packet taco seasoning mix

375g (12 ounces) bottled thick and chunky taco sauce

½ cup (125ml) water

10 stand 'n' stuff taco shells (140g)

1 cup (60g) finely shredded iceberg lettuce

1 medium carrot (120g), grated coarsely

125g (4 ounces) cherry tomatoes, quartered

½ cup (60g) coarsely grated cheddar cheese

½ cup loosely packed fresh coriander leaves (cilantro)

⅓ cup (80g) sour cream

1  Heat oil in a large frying pan over high heat; cook onion, stirring, until softened. Add chicken to pan; cook, stirring, until browned. Add seasoning mix to pan; cook, stirring, until fragrant. Add half the taco sauce and the water; cook over medium heat, stirring occasionally, for 7 minutes or until the mixture thickens. Remove from heat; season to taste.
2  Meanwhile, heat taco shells according to directions on packet.
3  Divide chicken mixture into taco shells; top with lettuce, carrot, tomato, cheese, coriander, sour cream and remaining taco sauce.

**nutritional count per taco**
- 35.9g total fat
- 13.3g saturated fat
- 2445kJ (585 cal)
- 29.7g carbohydrate
- 33.2g protein
- 6.7g fibre

# snapper Veracruz

**PREP + COOK TIME** 1 HOUR **SERVES** 4

This recipe is named after the large port city of Veracruz, where seafood is a specialty.

¼ cup (60ml) light olive oil

2 medium green capsicums (bell peppers) (400g), chopped coarsely

1 medium brown onion (150g), chopped coarsely

2 fresh small red thai (serrano) chillies, chopped finely

2 cloves garlic, crushed

¼ teaspoon ground white pepper

1 teaspoon ground cinnamon

4 medium tomatoes (600g), chopped coarsely

¾ cup (110g) pimiento-stuffed green olives, chopped coarsely

2 tablespoons rinsed, drained capers, chopped coarsely

1 tablespoon lemon juice

2 x 800g (1½-pound) whole snapper

lemon wedges, to serve

**1** Heat oil in a large frying pan over medium heat; cook capsicum, onion, chilli and garlic, stirring, for 5 minutes or until onion softens.
**2** Add pepper, cinnamon and tomato; simmer, uncovered, stirring occasionally, for 10 minutes or until tomato has broken down and sauce is thick. Stir in olives, capers and juice; season. Cool.
**3** Preheat oven to 180°C/350°F.
**4** Score fish three times on each side through the thickest part of the flesh; place fish in a large baking dish, season. Pour tomato mixture over fish.
**5** Transfer dish to oven; bake fish uncovered, for 30 minutes or until fish is cooked through. Serve with lemon wedges.

**nutritional count per serving**
► 19.7g total fat
► 3.5g saturated fat
► 1710kJ (409 cal)
► 8.1g carbohydrate
► 46.7g protein
► 5.5g fibre

# paprika and parmesan polenta with walnut and capsicum salsa

**PREP + COOK TIME** 1 HOUR (+ REFRIGERATION)  **SERVES** 6

You can use olive oil instead of the walnut oil, if you prefer.

20g (¾ ounce) butter

2 medium brown onions (300g), sliced thinly

1 tablespoon brown sugar

1 litre (4 cups) water

1⅓ cups (225g) polenta

2 teaspoons smoked paprika

1 tablespoon red wine vinegar

1 cup (80g) coarsely grated parmesan cheese

WALNUT CAPSICUM SALSA

2 large red capsicums (bell peppers) (700g)

1½ cups (150g) roasted walnuts, chopped coarsely

1 tablespoon red wine vinegar

¼ cup (60ml) walnut oil

1 clove garlic, crushed

½ cup coarsely chopped fresh flat-leaf parsley

⅓ cup coarsely chopped fresh coriander (cilantro)

**1** Melt butter in a medium frying pan over medium heat; cook onion, stirring, about 5 minutes or until softened. Add sugar and 2 tablespoons of the water; cook, stirring, for 5 minutes or until the onion caramelises. Cover to keep warm.

**2** Oil a deep 22cm (9-inch) round cake pan. Bring the remaining water to the boil in a medium saucepan. Gradually add polenta and paprika, stirring constantly. Simmer, stirring, for 8 minutes or until polenta thickens. Stir in vinegar and cheese.

**3** Spread half the polenta into pan. Spread onion mixture over polenta, then spread remaining polenta over onion. Cover; refrigerate until firm.

**4** Meanwhile, make walnut capsicum salsa.

**5** Turn polenta onto a board; cut into six wedges. Cook polenta, both sides, on a heated oiled grill plate (or grill or barbecue) until browned lightly and hot. Serve polenta with salsa.

**WALNUT AND CAPSICUM SALSA** Preheat grill (broiler). Quarter capsicums, discard seeds and membranes. Place capsicum, skin-side up, on an oven tray; grill until skin blisters and blackens. Cover capsicum pieces with plastic or paper for 5 minutes; peel away skin, then chop flesh coarsely. Combine capsicum and remaining ingredients in a small bowl; season.

nutritional count per serving
▸ 51.8g total fat
▸ 10.6g saturated fat
▸ 3210kJ (768 cal)
▸ 51.9g carbohydrate
▸ 21.2g protein
▸ 7.1g fibre

# chicken quesadillas with guacamole

**PREP + COOK TIME** 45 MINUTES  **SERVES** 4

1 tablespoon olive oil

1 small red onion (100g), chopped finely

2 cloves garlic, crushed

¼ teaspoon cayenne pepper

2 teaspoons ground cumin

1 medium red capsicum (bell pepper) (200g), chopped finely

1 medium green capsicum (bell pepper) (200g), chopped finely

3 cups (480g) shredded barbecued chicken

8 x 20cm (8-inch) flour tortillas

2 cups (240g) coarsely grated cheddar cheese

⅓ cup loosely packed fresh coriander leaves (cilantro)

### GUACAMOLE

2 large avocados (640g), chopped coarsely

½ small red onion (50g), chopped finely

1 large tomato (220g), seeded, chopped finely

2 tablespoons lime juice

1 tablespoon finely chopped fresh coriander (cilantro)

**1** Heat oil in a large frying pan; cook onion and garlic, stirring, until onion softens. Add spices and capsicums; cook, stirring, until capsicums soften. Remove from heat; stir in chicken. Season to taste.

**2** Place one tortilla on board; top with ¼ cup of the cheese, then a quarter of the chicken mixture and another ¼ cup of the cheese. Top with a second tortilla. Repeat with remaining tortillas, cheese and chicken mixture.

**3** Cook quesadillas, one at a time, in the same oiled pan, over medium heat, until golden brown both sides. Remove from pan; cover to keep warm while cooking remaining quesadillas.

**4** Meanwhile, make guacamole.

**5** Cut quesadillas into quarters; accompany with guacamole, coriander and, if you like, a dollop of sour cream.

**GUACAMOLE** Mash avocado in a medium bowl; stir in remaining ingredients. Season to taste.

**nutritional count per serving**
▶ 66g total fat
▶ 22.7g saturated fat
▶ 4393kJ (1051 cal)
▶ 54.3g carbohydrate
▶ 57.1g protein
▶ 6.7g fibre

# pork ribs with chorizo and smoked paprika

**PREP + COOK TIME** 2¼ HOURS  **SERVES** 4

1.5kg (3 pounds) american-style pork spareribs

4 cloves garlic, crushed

2 teaspoons smoked paprika

1 tablespoon olive oil

1 cured chorizo sausage (170g), sliced thinly

1 tablespoon olive oil, extra

1 medium red onion (170g), chopped coarsely

1 medium red capsicum (bell pepper) (200g), chopped coarsely

1 tablespoon brown sugar

800g (1½ pounds) canned chopped tomatoes

1 cup (250ml) chicken stock

**1** Cut between the bones of the pork ribs to separate into individual ribs. Combine garlic, paprika and oil in a small bowl; rub over ribs.

**2** Preheat oven to 160°C/325°F.

**3** Cook chorizo in a heated large flameproof baking dish, stirring, until browned lightly. Remove from dish with a slotted spoon; drain on absorbent paper.

**4** Cook ribs, in batches, in same dish until browned. Remove from dish; drain on absorbent paper.

**5** Add extra oil, onion and capsicum to dish; cook, stirring, until onion softens. Return ribs and chorizo to dish with sugar, tomatoes and stock; bring to the boil.

**6** Cover dish tightly with foil; cook, in oven, for 1 hour. Remove foil; cook for a further 30 minutes or until ribs are tender. Season to taste.

nutritional count per serving
▶ 38.5g total fat
▶ 11.4g saturated fat
▶ 2516kJ (602 cal)
▶ 15.6g carbohydrate
▶ 49.2g protein
▶ 4.1g fibre

# BEANS & RICE

## saffron rice with zucchini flowers

**PREP + COOK TIME** 30 MINUTES **SERVES** 4

The stem of zucchini is the baby zucchini attached to the flower. You need to cook about 1½ cups (300g) white long-grain rice for this recipe. Spread cooked rice on a flat tray and refrigerate, uncovered, overnight before using.

12 zucchini flowers, stem attached (240g)

45g (1½ ounces) butter

1 large red onion (300g), cut into wedges

2 teaspoons caraway seeds

1 clove garlic, crushed

4 cups (850g) cooked white long-grain rice

1 teaspoon ground turmeric

pinch saffron threads

¼ cup (20g) flaked almonds, roasted

1  Remove flowers from zucchini; discard stamens from flowers. Slice zucchini thinly.
2  Melt butter in a large frying pan over medium heat; cook onion, seeds and garlic, stirring, about 5 minutes or until onion softens. Add sliced zucchini; cook, stirring, until tender. Add rice, spices and zucchini flowers; cook, stirring, until hot. Stir in half the nuts; season to taste.
3  Serve sprinkled with remaining nuts.

nutritional count per serving
▸ 12.9g total fat
▸ 6.2g saturated fat
▸ 1747kJ (418 cal)
▸ 65.3g carbohydrate
▸ 8g protein
▸ 3.6g fibre

# mexican rice

PREP + COOK TIME 1 HOUR  SERVES 4

1 medium brown onion (150g), quartered

2 large tomatoes (440g), quartered

2 cloves garlic, unpeeled

2 tablespoons olive oil

½ teaspoon chilli powder

1½ cups (300g) white long-grain rice

2 cups (500ml) chicken stock

1 small carrot (70g), sliced thinly

½ cup (60g) frozen peas

125g (4 ounces) canned corn kernels,
rinsed, drained

⅓ cup coarsely chopped fresh coriander (cilantro)

1  Preheat oven to 200°C/400°F.
2  Place onion, tomato and garlic on an oiled oven tray; drizzle with half the oil. Roast, uncovered, for 25 minutes or until vegetables soften. When cool enough to handle, peel tomato and garlic.
3  Blend or process onion, tomato, garlic and chilli powder until smooth (you need 2 cups of puree).
4  Heat remaining oil in a medium saucepan over medium heat; cook rice, stirring, for 3 minutes. Add tomato mixture; cook, stirring, for 8 minutes or until almost all of the liquid is evaporated.
5  Add stock, carrot, peas and corn to pan; bring to the boil. Reduce heat; simmer, covered, over low heat, for 10 minutes or until rice is tender and liquid is absorbed. Remove from heat; stand, covered, for 10 minutes. Fluff rice with a fork; season to taste. Serve sprinkled with coriander.

**nutritional count per serving**
▶ 7.9g total fat
▶ 1.2g saturated fat
▶ 1739kJ (416 cal)
▶ 72.9g carbohydrate
▶ 10g protein
▶ 5.3g fibre

# refried beans

PREP + COOK TIME 1½ HOURS (+ STANDING) SERVES 6

1¾ cups (350g) dried kidney beans

1.5 litres (6 cups) water

1 small brown onion (80g), chopped coarsely

1 clove garlic, crushed

1 dried bay leaf

½ fresh small green chilli, chopped finely

2 tablespoons olive oil

1 small brown onion (80g), chopped finely

1 large tomato (220g), peeled, chopped finely

**1** Place beans in a medium bowl, cover with water; stand overnight. Drain.

**2** Combine beans, the water, coarsely chopped onion, garlic, bay leaf and chilli in a large saucepan; bring to the boil. Reduce heat; simmer, covered, for 1 hour or until beans are tender.

**3** Drain bean mixture over a heatproof bowl; discard bay leaf; reserve ½ cup of cooking liquid. Blend or process bean mixture with reserved cooking liquid until coarsely mashed.

**4** Heat oil in a large frying pan over medium heat; cook finely chopped onion, stirring, for 5 minutes or until onion softens. Add tomato; cook, stirring, until tomato softens. Stir in bean mixture; cook, stirring, over low heat, for 10 minutes or until thickened; season.

**SERVING SUGGESTION** Serve as a dip with corn chips or use as a vegetarian filling for tacos, quesadillas or burritos.

**nutritional count per serving**
- 7.2g total fat
- 1g saturated fat
- 1003kJ (240 cal)
- 23g carbohydrate
- 13.9g protein
- 13.4g fibre

Red beans and rice is a filling and budget-friendly dish. You need one trimmed corn cob to get the amount of corn kernels required for this recipe, or use the same amount of drained canned corn kernels or frozen corn kernels, if you prefer.

# red beans and rice

PREP + COOK TIME 1 HOUR  SERVES 4

2 rindless bacon slices (130g), chopped coarsely

1 medium brown onion (150g), chopped finely

2 cloves garlic, crushed

1 small red capsicum (bell pepper) (150g), chopped finely

1 tablespoon tomato paste

1 tablespoon red wine vinegar

1 teaspoon smoked paprika

2 cups (400g) white long-grain rice

1 dried bay leaf

1 cup (250ml) chicken stock

2¼ cups (560ml) water

410g (13 ounces) canned kidney beans, rinsed, drained

½ cup (80g) corn kernels

1 tablespoon lime juice

**1** Cook bacon in a heated large frying pan over high heat, stirring, until starting to crisp. Add onion, garlic and capsicum; cook, stirring, for 3 minutes or until onion softens.
**2** Add paste, vinegar and paprika; cook, stirring, for 1 minute. Add rice; cook, stirring, for 2 minutes.
**3** Add bay leaf, stock, the water and beans; bring to the boil. Reduce heat; simmer, covered, for 20 minutes. Add corn; cook, covered, for 5 minutes or until rice is tender. Remove from heat; stand, covered, for 5 minutes. Stir in juice; season to taste.

**SERVING SUGGESTION** Serve this as an accompaniment to grilled chicken, or any of the main meals in this book.

**nutritional count per serving**
▶ 3.3g total fat
▶ 1g saturated fat
▶ 2215kJ (530 cal)
▶ 99.3g carbohydrate
▶ 20.8g protein
▶ 7.1g fibre

# green rice

PREP + COOK TIME 1 HOUR  SERVES 4

1 large green capsicum (bell pepper) (350g)

2 medium brown onions (300g), quartered

4 cloves garlic, unpeeled

2 fresh small green chillies

¼ cup (60ml) olive oil

3 cups (750ml) chicken stock

⅓ cup each firmly packed fresh flat-leaf parsley and coriander (cilantro) leaves

1½ cups (300g) white long-grain rice

**1** Preheat oven to 200°C/400°F.

**2** Quarter capsicum; discard seeds and membranes. Place capsicum, onion, garlic and chilli on an oiled oven tray; drizzle with 1 tablespoon oil. Transfer to oven; roast, uncovered, for 25 minutes or until vegetables soften. When cool enough to handle, peel capsicum and garlic; discard stems from chillies.

**3** Blend or process capsicum, onion, garlic and chilli with 1 cup stock until combined.  Add herbs; blend or process until smooth.

**4** Heat remaining oil in a medium saucepan; cook rice, stirring, for 3 minutes or until rice is browned lightly. Stir in herb mixture and remaining stock; bring to the boil. Reduce heat; simmer, covered, for 15 minutes or until rice is tender and liquid is absorbed. Remove from heat; stand, covered, for 10 minutes. Fluff rice with a fork; season to taste.

**nutritional count per serving**

▶ 14.4g total fat

▶ 2.2g saturated fat

▶ 1839kJ (440 cal)

▶ 67.3g carbohydrate

▶ 9g protein

▶ 2.7g fibre

# drunken beans

**PREP + COOK TIME** 1¾ HOURS (+ STANDING) **SERVES** 4

1 cup (200g) dried pinto beans

3 rindless bacon slices (195g), chopped coarsely

1 medium brown onion (150g), chopped finely

1 clove garlic, crushed

1 teaspoon ground cumin

½ teaspoon cayenne pepper

1 tablespoon tomato paste

400g (12½ ounces) canned crushed tomatoes

1 cup (250ml) water

1 cup (250ml) beer

1 tablespoon worcestershire sauce

2 tablespoons brown sugar

**1** Place beans in a medium bowl, cover with water; stand overnight. Drain.

**2** Cook bacon, onion, garlic and spices in an oiled large saucepan over high heat, stirring, for 3 minutes or until onion softens.

**3** Add drained beans and remaining ingredients to pan; bring to the boil. Reduce heat; simmer, covered, for 1½ hours or until beans are just tender. Season to taste.

**nutritional count per serving**

▶ 4.8g total fat     ▶ 32.1g carbohydrate
▶ 1.5g saturated fat     ▶ 21.6g protein
▶ 1267kJ (303 cal)     ▶ 12.8g fibre

# SALSAS & SAUCES

## grilled corn and zucchini salsa

**PREP + COOK TIME** 30 MINUTES  **MAKES** 7 CUPS

2 corn cobs (800g), trimmed

100g (3 ounces) baby zucchini, halved lengthways

2 large avocados (640g), chopped coarsely

200g (6½ ounces) grape tomatoes, halved

1 medium red onion (170g), sliced thickly

¼ cup coarsely chopped fresh coriander (cilantro)

1 tablespoon sweet chilli sauce

⅓ cup (80ml) lime juice

2 fresh small red thai (serrano) chillies, sliced thinly

1  Cook corn and zucchini on a heated oiled grill plate (or grill or barbecue) until tender and browned lightly. When cool enough to handle, cut kernels from cobs.

2  Place corn and zucchini in a large bowl with avocado, tomato, onion and coriander. Add combined sauce, juice and chilli; toss gently to combine. Season to taste.

**SERVING SUGGESTION** Serve with grilled salmon or chicken, barbecued beef rump steak, or chicken or beef fajitas. This recipe makes enough for six servings.

**nutritional count per tablespoon**

► 1.3g total fat
► 0.3g saturated fat
► 84kJ (20 cal)
► 1.4g carbohydrate
► 0.5g protein
► 0.5g fibre

# hot sauce

**PREP + COOK TIME** 1½ HOURS (+ STANDING)  **MAKES** 3 CUPS

Hot sauce is the perfect condiment to use if you want to add extra spice to your meal. Spoon a little hot sauce on enchiladas, tacos or even scrambled eggs, if you like.

3 ancho chillies

1 cup (250ml) boiling water

6 medium ripe tomatoes (900g), chopped coarsely

4 cloves garlic, quartered

1 small brown onion (80g), chopped coarsely

3 whole cloves

2 tablespoons red wine vinegar

1 teaspoon dried thyme leaves

½ teaspoon dried oregano leaves

½ teaspoon ground cumin

2 tablespoons olive oil

**1**  Cover chillies with the boiling water in a small heatproof bowl; stand for 20 minutes.
**2**  Meanwhile, blend or process tomato until smooth. Transfer to a small bowl.
**3**  Discard stalks from chillies; blend or process chilli and soaking liquid with garlic, onion, cloves, vinegar, herbs and cumin until smooth.
**4**  Heat oil in a large frying pan; cook chilli mixture, stirring, until mixture boils. Add tomato; simmer, uncovered, stirring occasionally, for 1 hour or until reduced to about 3 cups. Season to taste; cool.

**nutritional count per tablespoon**
▶ 1g total fat          ▶ 0.6g carbohydrate
▶ 0.1g saturated fat    ▶ 0.3g protein
▶ 59kJ (14 cal)         ▶ 0.4g fibre

# mango and avocado salsa

**PREP TIME** 15 MINUTES  **MAKES** 2½ CUPS

1 medium mango (430g), chopped coarsely

1 large avocado (320g), chopped coarsely

1 small red onion (100g), chopped finely

1 small red capsicum (bell pepper) (150g), chopped finely

1 fresh small red thai (serrano) chilli, chopped finely

2 tablespoons lime juice

**1** Combine ingredients in a medium bowl; season to taste.

**SERVING SUGGESTION** Serve with roasted corn, grilled chicken or salmon fillets.

**nutritional count per tablespoon**

▶ 1.7g total fat    ▶ 1.6g carbohydrate
▶ 0.4g saturated fat    ▶ 0.4g protein
▶ 100kJ (24 cal)    ▶ 0.4g fibre

# black bean and mango salsa

PREP + COOK TIME 1¾ HOURS (+ STANDING) SERVES 6

| |
|---|
| 1 cup (200g) dried black beans |
| 1 lebanese cucumber (130g), seeded, sliced thinly |
| 1 medium mango (430g), chopped finely |
| 1 cup loosely packed fresh coriander leaves (cilantro) |

**SWEET CHILLI DRESSING**

| |
|---|
| 1 tablespoon olive oil |
| 1 tablespoon sweet chilli sauce |
| 1 tablespoon lime juice |

**1** Place beans in a medium bowl, cover with water; stand overnight. Drain.
**2** Cook beans in a medium saucepan of boiling water until tender; drain.
**3** Meanwhile, make sweet chilli dressing.
**4** Place beans in a medium bowl with dressing and remaining ingredients; toss gently to combine, season to taste.

**SWEET CHILLI DRESSING** Combine ingredients in a small bowl.

---

**nutritional count per serving**
▶ 9.9g total fat  ▶ 9.7g carbohydrate
▶ 1.5g saturated fat  ▶ 11.6g protein
▶ 790kJ (189 cal)  ▶ 7.8g fibre

# guacamole

**PREP TIME** 10 MINUTES  **MAKES** 2½ CUPS

Serve as a dip with corn chips; it also goes well with nachos, burritos and fajitas.

2 medium avocados (500g)

½ small red onion (50g), chopped finely

1 medium roma (egg) tomato (75g), seeded, chopped finely

1 tablespoon lime juice

¼ cup coarsely chopped fresh coriander (cilantro)

**1**  Mash avocados in a medium bowl; stir in remaining ingredients. Season to taste.

**nutritional count per tablespoon**
▸ 2.6g total fat
▸ 0.6g saturated fat
▸ 109kJ (26 cal)
▸ 0.2g carbohydrate
▸ 0.3g protein
▸ 0.2g fibre

# SWEET TREATS

## flan de café

**PREP + COOK TIME** 50 MINUTES (+ REFRIGERATION) **MAKES** 6

¾ cup (165g) caster (superfine) sugar

¾ cup (180ml) water

6 eggs

⅓ cup (75g) caster (superfine) sugar, extra

2 tablespoons coffee-flavoured liqueur

1 tablespoon instant coffee granules

1 tablespoon water, extra

1½ cups (375ml) milk

300ml thickened (heavy) cream

**1** Preheat oven to 160°C/325°F.
**2** Stir sugar and the water in a medium saucepan over heat, without boiling, until sugar dissolves. Bring to the boil; boil, uncovered, without stirring, for 5 minutes or until mixture is golden brown. Pour evenly into six 1-cup (250ml) ovenproof dishes.
**3** Whisk eggs and extra sugar together in a medium bowl; stir in liqueur and combined coffee and the extra water.
**4** Bring milk and cream to the boil in a medium saucepan. Remove from heat; allow bubbles to subside. Gradually whisk milk mixture into egg mixture; strain into jug.
**5** Place dishes in a baking dish; pour custard into dishes. Pour enough boiling water into baking dish to come halfway up sides of dishes.
**6** Bake flans for 30 minutes or until just set. Remove dishes from water; cool to room temperature. Refrigerate overnight.
**7** Turn flans onto serving plates, serve with whipped cream and sprinkled with orange zest, if you like.

**nutritional count per flan**
- ▶ 26.9g total fat
- ▶ 15.9g saturated fat
- ▶ 1363kJ (326 cal)
- ▶ 48.1g carbohydrate
- ▶ 10g protein
- ▶ 0.1g fibre

# grilled bananas with coconut syrup

**PREP + COOK TIME** 15 MINUTES  **SERVES** 4

We used Malibu, a rum-based coconut liqueur, for this recipe. Serve with whipped cream or ice-cream, if you like.

⅓ cup (80ml) water

¼ cup (55g) firmly packed brown sugar

¼ cup (60ml) coconut-flavoured liqueur

4 large ripe bananas (920g)

2 teaspoons finely grated lime rind

¼ cup (20g) shredded coconut, toasted

**1** Stir the water and sugar in a small saucepan over heat, without boiling, until sugar dissolves; bring to the boil. Reduce heat; simmer, uncovered, without stirring, for 3 minutes or until syrup thickens slightly. Remove from heat; stir in liqueur.

**2** Split bananas lengthways; brush about a quarter of the syrup mixture over the cut-sides of bananas.

**3** Cook bananas, cut-side down, on a heated lightly oiled grill plate (or grill or barbecue) until browned lightly and heated through.

**4** Meanwhile, heat remaining syrup mixture in a small saucepan until hot. Remove from heat; stir in rind.

**5** Serve hot bananas drizzled with syrup; sprinkle with coconut.

**nutritional count per serving**
- 3.5g total fat
- 2.6g saturated fat
- 1116kJ (267 cal)
- 47g carbohydrate
- 2.6g protein
- 3.7g fibre

# fried sweet pastries

**PREP + COOK TIME** 45 MINUTES (+ STANDING) **MAKES** 16

**4 eggs**

¼ **cup (55g) caster (superfine) sugar**

1¾ **cups (260g) plain (all-purpose) flour**

½ **cup (75g) self-raising flour**

½ **teaspoon salt**

**vegetable oil, for shallow-frying**

1¼ **cups (275g) caster (superfine) sugar, extra**

1½ **teaspoons ground cinnamon**

**1** Beat eggs and sugar in a small bowl with an electric mixer until thick and creamy. Transfer mixture to a large bowl; stir in sifted flours and salt, in two batches. Knead dough on a floured surface until smooth and no longer sticky. Wrap in plastic wrap; stand for 20 minutes.

**2** Divide dough into 16 portions. Roll each portion on a floured surface into 12cm (4¾-inch) rounds.

**3** Heat oil in a large frying pan; shallow-fry pastries, one at a time, turning once, until browned lightly. Drain on absorbent paper.

**4** Toss hot pastries in combined extra sugar and cinnamon. Serve warm or cold.

**nutritional count per pastry**

▶ 5.9g total fat  ▶ 32.2g carbohydrate
▶ 1g saturated fat  ▶ 3.9g protein
▶ 548kJ (131 cal)  ▶ 0.8g fibre

# royal eggs

PREP + COOK TIME 50 MINUTES (+ COOLING) SERVES 4

12 egg yolks

2 teaspoons baking powder

1 teaspoon water

1 teaspoon melted butter

CINNAMON SYRUP

2 cups (440g) caster (superfine) sugar

1 cup (250ml) water

3 cinnamon sticks, broken

½ cup (125ml) dry sherry

2 tablespoons lime juice

⅓ cup (50g) raisins

⅓ cup (50g) pine nuts, roasted

1 Preheat oven to 160°C/325°F. Grease a deep 20cm (8-inch) square cake pan; line base with baking paper, grease paper.

2 Beat egg yolks and baking powder in a small bowl with an electric mixer until thick and creamy; fold in the water and butter. Pour mixture into pan.

3 Place pan in a baking dish; add enough boiling water to dish to come half way up sides of pan.

4 Bake cake for 15 minutes or until firm. Remove pan from water; stand for 10 minutes.

5 Meanwhile, make cinnamon syrup.

6 Carefully turn cake onto a board; cut into squares. Place squares in a deep heatproof dish, pour over hot syrup; stand until syrup is cool.

CINNAMON SYRUP Stir sugar, the water, cinnamon, sherry and juice in a medium saucepan, over medium-high heat, without boiling, until sugar dissolves; bring to the boil. Reduce heat; simmer, uncovered, without stirring, for 3 minutes or until syrup is thickened slightly. Remove from heat; stir in raisins and nuts.

nutritional count per serving

▶ 26.8g total fat

▶ 7g saturated fat

▶ 1488kJ (356 cal)

▶ 120g carbohydrate

▶ 11.4g protein

▶ 1.3g fibre

# coconut and pineapple chimichangas

**PREP + COOK TIME** 45 MINUTES **MAKES** 16

⅔ cup (180g) canned crushed pineapple, drained

½ cup (85g) finely chopped raisins

⅓ cup (110g) apricot jam

2 teaspoons ground cinnamon

½ cup (40g) shredded coconut

8 x 15cm (6-inch) flour tortillas

vegetable oil, for deep-frying

1 tablespoon icing (confectioners') sugar

1 Combine pineapple, raisins, jam, cinnamon and coconut in a medium bowl.

2 Heat tortillas according to instructions on packet.

3 Divide pineapple mixture evenly between warmed tortillas. Roll tortillas up firmly, folding in sides; secure with toothpicks.

4 Heat oil in a large frying pan; deep-fry tortilla rolls, in batches, until browned lightly. Drain on absorbent paper. Remove toothpicks.

5 Dust chimichangas with sifted icing sugar. Cut each chimichanga in half; serve with ice-cream or whipped cream, if you like.

**nutritional count per chimichanga**
▶ 4.1g total fat
▶ 1.7g saturated fat
▶ 427kJ (102 cal)
▶ 14.9g carbohydrate
▶ 1.2g protein
▶ 1.4g fibre

# mexican wedding cookies

**PREP + COOK TIME** 55 MINUTES (+ REFRIGERATION)  **MAKES** 34

250g (8 ounces) butter, softened

¾ cup (165g) caster (superfine) sugar

2 cups (300g) plain (all-purpose) flour

½ cup (75g) finely chopped blanched almonds

½ cup (60g) finely chopped pecans

1 tablespoon finely grated orange rind

1 teaspoon vanilla extract

1 egg yolk

¼ cup (40g) icing (confectioners') sugar

**1** Preheat oven to 180°C/350°F. Line oven trays with baking paper.

**2** Beat butter and caster sugar in a small bowl with an electric mixer until light and fluffy. Stir in sifted flour, nuts, rind, extract and egg yolk.

**3** Shape level tablespoons of dough into rectangles; place biscuits, about 2.5cm (1-inch) apart, on trays. Cover; refrigerate for 30 minutes.

**4** Bake biscuits for 25 minutes. Stand on trays for 5 minutes before transferring to wire racks to cool. Dust with sifted icing sugar.

**nutritional count per cookie**

▶ 8.8g total fat ▶ 12.7g carbohydrate

▶ 4.2g saturated fat ▶ 1.7g protein

▶ 489kJ (117 cal) ▶ 0.7g fibre

# poached guavas in spicy syrup

**PREP + COOK TIME** 1 HOUR (+ COOLING & REFRIGERATION) **SERVES** 4

1 lime

1½ cups (330g) caster (superfine) sugar

1 cinnamon stick

6 whole cloves

2½ cups (625ml) water

4 medium pink guavas (720g)

½ teaspoon vanilla extract

**1**  Using a vegetable peeler, peel rind thinly from lime; cut rind into thin strips. Squeeze 1 tablespoon juice from lime.

**2**  Combine rind, juice, sugar, cinnamon, cloves and the water in a medium saucepan; stir over medium heat, without boiling, until sugar dissolves. Simmer, covered, for 20 minutes.

**3**  Peel guavas; cut into quarters, discard seeds.

**4**  Add guavas to syrup; simmer, covered loosely, for 10 minutes or until guavas are tender. Cool guavas in syrup.

**5**  Remove guavas from syrup; place in a medium heatproof bowl. Strain syrup through a fine sieve; discard cinnamon and cloves.

**6**  Return syrup to same pan; simmer, uncovered, for 10 minutes or until reduced to about 1¼ cups. Remove pan from heat; stir in vanilla. Pour syrup over guavas; cool. Cover; refrigerate.

**7**  Serve guavas and syrup with yoghurt, whipped cream or ice-cream, if you like.

nutritional count per serving
▶ 0.5g total fat
▶ 0.1g saturated fat
▶ 142kJ (34 cal)
▶ 3.4g carbohydrate
▶ 0.7g protein
▶ 5.1g fibre

**nutritional count per serving**
▶ 12.5g total fat
▶ 5.7g saturated fat
▶ 1430kJ (342 cal)
▶ 55.1g carbohydrate
▶ 7.3g protein
▶ 2.4g fibre

On January 6, this fruit studded bread, commonly known as the 'round bread of the kings', celebrates the occasion when the Three Kings visited Jesus.

# three kings bread

**PREP + COOK TIME** 1 HOUR (+ STANDING) **SERVES** 12

1 tablespoon (14g) dried yeast

1 teaspoon caster (superfine) sugar

¼ cup (60ml) warm water

2½ cups (375g) plain (all-purpose) flour

1 teaspoon salt

100g (3 ounces) butter, chopped finely

¼ cup (55g) caster (superfine) sugar, extra

2 teaspoons each finely grated orange and lemon rind

2 eggs, beaten lightly

4 egg yolks

¼ cup (60g) coarsely chopped glacé figs

¼ cup (60g) coarsely chopped glacé apricots

¼ cup (40g) coarsely chopped raisins

¼ cup (25g) coarsely chopped roasted walnuts

1 egg, extra, beaten lightly

1 slice (40g) glacé orange, chopped coarsely

1 tablespoon coarsely chopped roasted walnuts, extra

**ORANGE ICING**

1¼ cups (200g) icing (confectioners') sugar

2 tablespoons orange juice

**1** Combine yeast, sugar and the water in a small bowl. Cover; stand in a warm place for 10 minutes or until mixture is frothy.

**2** Sift flour and salt into a large bowl; rub in butter. Stir in extra sugar and rind. Combine yeast mixture, eggs and egg yolks in a medium bowl; stir into flour mixture, mix to a soft dough.

**3** Knead dough on a floured surface for 10 minutes or until smooth and elastic. Place dough in a large oiled bowl. Cover; stand in a warm place for 1 hour or until dough doubles in size.

**4** Toss figs, apricots, raisins and nuts in an extra 1 tablespoon of plain flour, breaking up any chunks of fruit. Turn dough onto a floured surface, add fruit and nut mixture; knead until smooth.

**5** Roll dough into a 48cm (19¼-inch) log; shape log into a ring, press ends together firmly. Place ring on a greased oven tray (place around a greased round 9cm (3¾-inch) ovenproof dish so the dough ring keeps its shape during cooking). Cover; stand in a warm place for 50 minutes or until dough doubles in size.

**6** Preheat oven to 200°C/400°F.

**7** Brush ring all over with extra egg; bake for 10 minutes. Reduce oven temperature to 180°C/350°F. Bake bread for 15 minutes. Place bread on a wire rack over a tray, stand 30 minutes.

**8** Make orange icing.

**9** Pour icing over bread; decorate with glacé orange and sprinkle with extra nuts.

**ORANGE ICING** Combine sifted icing sugar and juice in a small jug.

# churros

PREP + COOK TIME 30 MINUTES  MAKES 35

| 1 cup (250ml) water |
| 1 tablespoon caster (superfine) sugar |
| 90g (3 ounces) butter, chopped coarsely |
| 1 cup (150g) plain (all-purpose) flour |
| 2 eggs |
| vegetable oil, for deep-frying |

**ANISEED SUGAR**

| 5 star anise |
| ½ cup (110g) caster (superfine) sugar |

**1**  Make aniseed sugar.

**2**  Bring the water, sugar and butter to the boil in a medium saucepan. Add sifted flour; beat with a wooden spoon over high heat until mixture comes away from the base and side of the pan to form a smooth ball. Transfer mixture to a small bowl; beat in eggs, one at a time, with an electric mixer until mixture becomes glossy.

**3**  Spoon mixture into a piping bag fitted with a 1cm (½-inch) fluted tube.

**4**  Heat oil in a large saucepan; pipe 6cm (2¼-inch) lengths of batter into the oil (cut off lengths with a sharp knife or oiled scissors). Deep-fry churros, in batches, for 6 minutes or until browned lightly and crisp. Drain churros on absorbent paper.

**5**  Roll churros in aniseed sugar. Serve warm.

**ANISEED SUGAR**  Blend or process ingredients until ground finely.

**nutritional count per churro**
▶ 3.4g total fat      ▶ 6.8g carbohydrate
▶ 1.6g saturated fat  ▶ 0.9g protein
▶ 247kJ (59 cal)      ▶ 0.2g fibre

# strawberry and peach tequila popsicles

**PREP TIME** 30 MINUTES (+ FREEZING)  **MAKES** 12

3 medium peaches (450g), chopped coarsely

¼ cup (65g) grated palm sugar

⅓ cup (80ml) tequila

1 tablespoon citrus-flavoured liqueur

1 tablespoon lemon juice

500g (1 pound) strawberries, chopped coarsely

**1** Blend or process peaches until smooth. Push peaches through a sieve into a medium bowl; stir in half the sugar, half the tequila, and all the liqueur and juice.

**2** Divide half the peach mixture into 12 x ⅓ cup (80ml) ice-block moulds (or paper cups); refrigerate remaining peach mixture. Freeze ice-block moulds for 30 minutes or until surface is firm.

**3** Blend or process strawberries until smooth. Push strawberries through a sieve into a medium bowl; stir in remaining sugar and tequila.

**4** Press paddle pop stick firmly into each popsicle. Divide half the strawberry mixture into moulds; refrigerate remaining strawberry mixture. Freeze ice-block moulds for 30 minutes or until surface is firm.

**5** Divide remaining peach mixture into moulds; freeze for 30 minutes or until surface is firm.

**6** Divide remaining strawberry mixture into moulds; freeze popsicles overnight.

**TIP** We used Cointreau, but you can use your favourite citrus-flavoured liqueur.

nutritional count per popsicle
- ▶ 0.1g total fat
- ▶ 0g saturated fat
- ▶ 322kJ (77 cal)
- ▶ 12.5g carbohydrate
- ▶ 1g protein
- ▶ 1.4g fibre

# GLOSSARY

**ALLSPICE** also called jamaican pepper or pimento; tastes like a combination of nutmeg, cumin, clove and cinnamon – all spices. Sold whole or ground.

**ALMONDS**
*blanched* brown skins removed.
*flaked* paper-thin slices.

**AVOCADO** a tree native to Mexico and Central America; also refers to the fruit, a large berry that contains a single seed.

**BAKING PAPER** also called parchment paper or baking parchment; a silicone-coated paper used to line baking pans and oven trays so food won't stick, making removal easy.

**BAKING POWDER** a raising agent consisting mainly of two parts cream of tartar to one part bicarbonate of soda. Also available gluten free.

**BAY LEAVES** aromatic leaves from the bay tree available fresh or dried; adds a strong, slightly peppery flavour.

**BEANS**
*black* also called turtle beans or black kidney beans; an earthy-flavoured dried bean completely different from the better-known chinese black beans (fermented soya beans). Used mostly in Mexican and South American cooking.
*borlotti* also called roman or pink beans, can be eaten fresh or dried. Interchangeable with pinto beans due to their similarity in appearance - pale pink or beige with dark red streaks.
*green* also known as french or string beans (although the tough string they once had has generally been bred out of them); this long thin fresh bean is consumed in its entirety once cooked.
*kidney* medium-sized red bean, slightly floury in texture yet sweet in flavour; sold dried or canned, it's often found in bean mixes.
*mexican-style* a canned mixture of either kidney or pinto beans cooked with tomato, peppers, onion, garlic and various spices.
*pinto* similar to borlotti, a plump, kidney-shaped, beige bean speckled with brown.
*refried* pinto beans, cooked twice – soaked and boiled, then mashed and fried, traditionally in lard. A Mexican staple, frijoles refritos or refried beans are available canned in supermarkets.

**BEEF**
*chuck* inexpensive cut from the neck and shoulder area.

*fillet* also known as a tenderloin fillet; an expensive and extremely tender cut.
*rump* a tender, boneless cut taken from the upper part of the hindquarter.

**BLOOD ORANGE** a virtually seedless citrus fruit with blood-red flesh; it has a sweet, non-acidic pulp and juice with slight berry overtones. The rind is not as bitter as an ordinary orange.

**BUTTER** we use salted butter unless stated otherwise; 125g is equal to 1 stick (4 ounces).

**BUTTERMILK** originally the term given to the slightly sour liquid left after butter was churned from cream, today it is made similarly to yoghurt from no-fat or low-fat milk to which specific bacterial cultures have been added. Sold alongside fresh milk products in supermarkets; despite the implication of its name, it's low in fat.

**BUTTON MUSHROOMS** small, cultivated white mushrooms with a mild flavour.

**CAPERS** the grey-green buds of a warm climate (usually Mediterranean) shrub, sold either dried and salted or pickled in a vinegar brine. Capers should be rinsed before using.

**CAPSICUM** also known as pepper or bell pepper; belongs to the same family as hot chillies but does not contain heat. Found in red, green, yellow, orange or purplish-black varieties. Discard seeds and membranes before use.

**CARAWAY SEEDS** small dried seed from a member of the parsley family; has a sweet, tangy, anise flavour.

**CAYENNE PEPPER** a long, thin-fleshed, extremely hot red chilli that is usually sold dried and ground.

**CHEESE**
*cheddar* semi-hard, yellow to off-white cheese aged between nine months and two years; the flavour becomes sharper with time. It has a slightly crumbly texture if properly matured.
*cream* commonly called Philadelphia or Philly; a soft cow's-milk cheese, its fat content ranges from 14% to 33%.
*goat's* made from goat's milk, has an earthy, strong taste. Available in soft, crumbly and firm textures, in various shapes and sizes, and sometimes rolled in ash or herbs.

*parmesan* also known as parmigiano, parmesan is a hard, grainy cow's-milk cheese that originated in the Parma region of Italy. The curd is salted in brine for a month before being aged up to two years in humid conditions.

**CHICKEN**
*breast fillet* breast halved, skinned and boned.
*drumstick* the leg with the skin and bone intact.
*thigh cutlet* thigh with the skin and centre bone intact; sometimes found skinned with the bone intact.

**CHILLI**
*ancho* mild, dried chillies commonly used in Mexican cooking.
*chipotle* pronounced cheh-pote-lay. The name used for jalapeño chillies once they've been dried and smoked. Having a deep, intensely smoky flavour, rather than a searing heat, chipotles are dark brown, almost black in colour and wrinkled in appearance.
*green* any unripened chilli; also some varieties that are ripe when green, such as jalapeño, habanero or serrano.
*jalapeño* pronounced hah-lah-pain-yo. Fairly hot, medium-sized, plump, dark green chilli; available pickled in cans or bottled, and fresh, from greengrocers.
*long* available both fresh and dried and as red, green or orange/yellow; a generic term used for any moderately hot, long (about 6cm to 8cm), thin chilli.
*pasilla* medium hot, dried chillies; ground chilli powder can be substituted.
*red thai (serrano)* also known as 'scuds'; small, very hot and bright red in colour. Substitute with fresh serrano or habanero chillies.

**CHOCOLATE, DARK** also known as semi-sweet or luxury chocolate; made of a high percentage of cocoa liquor and cocoa butter, and a little added sugar.

**CHORIZO** sausage of Spanish origin, made of coarsely ground pork and highly seasoned with garlic and chilli. They are deeply smoked, very spicy and dry-cured so that they do not need cooking. Also available raw (fresh).

**CINNAMON** dried inner bark of the shoots of the cinnamon tree; available both in the piece (called sticks or quills) and ground into powder. One of the world's most common spices.

**CLOVES** dried flower buds of a tropical tree; can be used whole or in ground form. They have a strong scent and taste so should be used sparingly.

**COCONUT, SHREDDED** unsweetened thin strips of dried coconut flesh.

**CORIANDER** also known as pak chee, cilantro or chinese parsley; bright-green leafy herb with a pungent aroma and flavour. Both the stems and roots of coriander are used in cooking; wash well before using. Coriander seeds are also available dried and sold either whole or ground; these should not be substituted for fresh coriander as the tastes are completely different.

**CORNFLOUR (CORNSTARCH)** used as a thickening agent. Available made from wheat or 100% corn (maize).

**CREAM**
*pouring* also called fresh or pure cream; contains no additives and has a minimum fat content of 35%.
*sour* a thick, commercially cultured sour cream with a minimum fat content of 35%.
*thick (double)* a dolloping cream with a minimum fat content of 45%.
*thickened (heavy)* a whipping cream containing a thickener. Has a minimum fat content of 35%.

**CUCUMBER, LEBANESE** short, slender and thin-skinned cucumber. Probably the most popular variety because of its tender, edible skin, tiny, yielding seeds, and sweet, fresh and flavoursome taste.

**CUMIN** a spice also called zeera or comino; resembling caraway in size, cumin is the dried seed of a plant related to the parsley family. It has a spicy, almost curry-like flavour, and is traditionally used in Mexican dishes. It is also available ground.

**DILL** also known as dill weed; it has an anise/celery sweetness. Used dried, in seed form or ground, or fresh – the distinctive feathery, frond-like fresh leaves are grassier and more subtle than the dried version or the seeds (which slightly resemble caraway in flavour).

**EGGS** we use large (60g) chicken eggs unless stated otherwise. If a recipe calls for raw or barely cooked eggs, exercise caution if there is a salmonella problem in your area. The risk is greater for those who are pregnant, elderly or very young.

**FIGS** are best eaten in peak season, at the height of summer. Vary in skin and flesh colour according to type not ripeness. Figs are also glacéd (candied), dried or canned in sugar syrup.

**FLOUR**
*plain (all-purpose)* unbleached wheat flour is the best for baking: the gluten content ensures a strong dough, which produces a light result. Also used as a thickening agent in sauces and gravies.
*self-raising* all-purpose plain or wholemeal flour with baking powder and salt added; make at home in the proportion of 1 cup flour to 2 teaspoons baking powder.

**GUAVA** a round or pear-shaped tropical fruit varying in size. It is thin-skinned with an aromatic, sharp-sweet flesh. Varieties include pink guava, which is high in lycopene. Guavas are eaten fresh and used for creamy desserts, a jelly preserve, and a stiff paste to serve with cheese. Available fresh and canned.

**LAMB SHANK** forequarter leg; sometimes sold as drumsticks or frenched shanks if the gristle and narrow end of the bone are discarded and the remaining meat trimmed.

**LETTUCE**
*cos* also known as romaine lettuce; the traditional caesar salad lettuce. Long, with leaves ranging from dark green on the outside to almost white near the core; the leaves have a stiff centre rib giving a slight cupping effect to the leaf on either side.
*iceberg* a heavy, firm, round lettuce with tightly packed leaves and crisp texture; the most common 'family' lettuce used in sandwiches as well as salads.

**LIQUEUR/SPIRITS**
*coconut-flavoured* we use Malibu.
*orange-flavoured* we use Cointreau.
*tequila* colourless alcoholic liquor of Mexican origin made from the fermented sap of the agave, a succulent desert plant.

**MANGO** tropical fruit originally from India and South-East Asia. Has a skin colour ranging from green to yellow and deep red; its fragrant, deep yellow flesh surrounds a large flat seed. They can be used in curries and salsas, or pureed for ice-cream, smoothies or mousse. Mango cheeks are available canned in light syrup.

**MUSTARD, DIJON** also called french mustard. A pale brown, creamy, fairly mild mustard.

**NUTMEG** a strong and pungent spice from the dried nut of an evergreen tree native to Indonesia. Usually available ground but the flavour is more intense from a whole nut, so it's best to grate your own with a fine grater. Often included in mixed spice mixtures.

**OIL**
*olive* made from ripened olives. Extra virgin and virgin are the first and second press, respectively, of the olives and are therefore considered the best; the 'extra light' or 'light' name on other types refers to taste not fat levels.
*peanut* pressed from ground peanuts; the most commonly used oil in Asian cooking because of its high smoke point (capacity to handle high heat without burning).
*vegetable* sourced from plant rather than animal fats.
*walnut* pressed from ground walnuts.

**ONION**
*brown and white* are interchangeable, however, white onions have a more pungent flesh.
*green* also known as scallion or, incorrectly, shallot. An immature onion picked before the bulb has formed, having a long, bright-green edible stalk.
*red* also known as spanish, red spanish or bermuda onion; a sweet-flavoured, large, purple-red onion.

**PAPRIKA** ground dried sweet red capsicum (bell pepper); there are many grades and types available, including sweet, hot, mild and smoked.

**PEPPERCORNS, BLACK** cooked and dried unripe fruit of the pepper plant.

**PINE NUTS** also known as pignoli; not a nut but a small, cream-coloured kernel from pine cones. Best roasted before use.

**PINEAPPLE** a tropical plant with edible fruit; pineapples are consumed fresh, cooked, juiced or preserved.

**POLENTA** also known as cornmeal; a flour-like cereal ground from dried corn (maize). Also the dish made from it.

**POMEGRANATE** Dark-red, leathery-skinned fresh fruit about the size of an orange. The individual cells contain seed kernels that are surrounded by an edible juice-filled sac (pulp).

**PORK**
*american-style spareribs* well-trimmed mid-loin ribs.
*loin* from the back area.
*neck* sometimes called pork scotch, boneless cut from the foreloin.

**RAISINS** dried sweet grapes (traditionally muscatel grapes).

**ROASTING/TOASTING** nuts and dried coconut can be roasted in the oven to restore their fresh flavour and release aromatic oils; spread evenly onto an oven tray, roast in a moderate oven about 5 minutes. Desiccated coconut, pine nuts and sesame seeds roast more evenly if stirred over low heat in a heavy-based frying pan; their natural oils help them turn golden.

**SAFFRON** available in strands or ground; imparts a yellow-orange colour to food once infused. Quality varies greatly; the best is the most expensive spice in the world. Store in the freezer.

**SALSA** the Spanish word for sauce but generally used in cooking to describe any raw or cooked Mexican sauce. Served also as a salad or dip. Raw, it is called 'salsa cruda' or 'salsa fresca'; there are myriad cooked salsas and most are named after their colour or content.

**SASHIMI** fish sold as sashimi has to meet stringent guidelines regarding its handling. We suggest you seek local advice from authorities before eating any raw seafood.

**SAUCE**
*hot* a chilli-infused sauce; use sparingly, increasing the quantity to suit your taste.
*sweet chilli* a mild, thai-style sauce made from red chillies, sugar, garlic and vinegar.
*Tabasco* brand-name of an extremely fiery sauce made from vinegar, hot red chillies and salt.
*worcestershire* a dark brown spicy condiment made from garlic, soy sauce, tamarind, anchovies, onions, molasses, lime, vinegar and other seasonings.

**SEAFOOD**
*cod, salted* a white fish that has been preserved by drying after salting.
*salmon* has a red-pink firm flesh with a moist delicate flavour and few bones.
*scallops* a bivalve mollusc with a fluted shell valve; we use scallops that have the coral (roe) removed. Available on the half-shell or shelled.

*snapper* small, firm-fleshed, distinct-tasting fish sold whole; good for any kind of cooking method. There are a number of varieties, including red, pink and yellowtail snapper.
*tuna* has a reddish, firm flesh that is slightly dry with no bones. Varieties include bluefin, yellowfin, skipjack or albacore; substitute with swordfish.
*white fish* means non-oily fish. This category includes bream, flathead, ling, whiting, snapper, jewfish and redfish. Remove any small bones with tweezers.

**SILVER BEET (SWISS CHARD)** also known, incorrectly, as spinach; has fleshy stalks and large leaves, both of which can be prepared as for spinach.

**SPINACH** also known as english spinach. Baby spinach leaves are best eaten raw in salads; the larger leaves should be added last to dishes and cooked until barely wilted.

**STALE BREADCRUMBS** made by grating or processing one- or two-day-old bread.

**STAR ANISE** a dried star-shaped pod whose seeds have an astringent aniseed flavour; commonly used to flavour stocks and marinades.

**STOCK** as a guide, 1 teaspoon of stock powder or 1 small crumbled stock cube or 1 portion stock concentrate mixed with 1 cup water will give a fairly strong stock. Be aware of the high salt and fat content of some stocks.

**SUGAR**
*caster (superfine)* finely granulated table sugar.
*icing* also known as confectioners' sugar or powdered sugar; pulverised granulated sugar crushed together with a small amount of cornflour.
*light brown* a soft, finely granulated sugar containing molasses, which gives it its characteristic colour and flavour.
*palm* also called nam tan pip, jaggery, jawa or gula melaka; made from the sap of the sugar palm tree. Light brown to black in colour and usually sold in rock-hard cakes; substitute with brown sugar.
*raw* natural brown granulated sugar.
*white* a coarse, granulated table sugar, also known as crystal sugar.

**TACO SEASONING MIX** packaged seasoning meant to duplicate the mild Mexican sauce made from oregano, cumin, chillies and other spices.

**TOMATILLO** also called mexican green tomato or husk tomato. The fruit looks like a small green tomato covered in a papery husk; it has a thin, bright green skin and a tart, lemony-herb flavour. Tomatillos can ripen to yellow but are generally used while still green and quite firm.

**TOMATOES**
*canned* whole peeled tomatoes in natural juices; available crushed, chopped or diced. Use undrained.
*cherry* also known as tiny tim or tom thumb tomatoes, small and round.
*egg (plum)* also called roma; smallish, oval-shaped tomatoes.
*grape* about the size of a grape; they can be oblong, pear or grape-shaped and are often used whole in salads or eaten as a snack.
*paste* triple-concentrated tomato puree.

**TORTILLA** thin, round, unleavened bread originating in Mexico; available frozen, fresh or vacuum-packed. Tortillas can be made from either wheat flour or from corn (maize meal).

**TURMERIC** also called kamin; is a rhizome related to galangal and ginger. Must be grated or pounded to release its acrid aroma and pungent flavour; known for the golden colour it imparts.

**VANILLA EXTRACT** made by extracting the flavour from the vanilla bean pod; the pods are soaked, usually in alcohol, to capture the authentic flavour.

**VINEGAR**
*balsamic* made from the juice of trebbiano grapes; it is a deep rich brown colour with a sweet and sour flavour.
*cider (apple cider)* made from crushed fermented apples.
*red wine* based on a blend of fermented red wine.
*white wine* made from a blend of white wines.

**WATERCRESS** a slightly peppery, dark-green leafy vegetable. Highly perishable, so must be used as soon as possible after purchase.

**WHITE RICE** hulled and polished rice, can be short, medium or long-grained.

**ZUCCHINI** also known as courgette; small, pale- or dark-green, yellow or white vegetable belonging to the squash family. Harvested when young, its edible flowers can be stuffed and then deep-fried or oven-baked.

# INDEX

This book is published in 2014 by Octopus Publishing Group Limited
based on materials licensed to it by Bauer Media Books, Australia

Bauer Media Books is a division of Bauer Media Pty Limited.

54 Park St, Sydney; GPO Box 4088, Sydney, NSW 2001, Australia

phone (+61) 2 9282 8618; fax (+61) 2 9126 3702

www.awwcookbooks.com.au

MEDIA GROUP

BAUER MEDIA BOOKS

Publisher – Jo Runciman

Editorial & food director – Pamela Clark

Director of sales, marketing & rights – Brian Cearnes

Creative director & designer– Hieu Chi Nguyen

Art director – Hannah Blackmore

Senior editor – Wendy Bryant

Food editor – Emma Braz

Published and Distributed in the United Kingdom by Octopus Publishing Group

Endeavour House

189 Shaftesbury Avenue

London WC2H 8JY

phone (+44) (0) 207 632 5400; fax (+44) (0) 207 632 5405

info@octopus-publishing.co.uk;

www.octopusbooks.co.uk

Printed by Toppan Printing Co., China

International foreign language rights, Brian Cearnes, Bauer Media Books bcearnes@bauer-media.com.au

A catalogue record for this book is available from the British Library.
ISBN: 978 174245 432 0 (paperback)

© Bauer Media Pty Ltd  2014
ABN 18 053 273 546

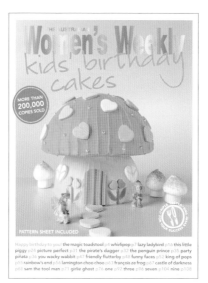

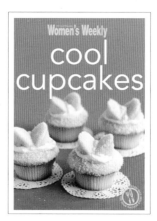